Our State
GREATEST Hits
VOLUME I

copyright © 2023 by *Our State* magazine.
All rights reserved.
Published by *Our State* magazine, Mann Media, Inc.
PO Box 4552, Greensboro, NC 27404
(800) 948-1409 | ourstate.com
Printed in the United States by Lakeside Book Company

No part of this book may be used or reproduced
in any manner without written permission.

EDITOR IN CHIEF: Elizabeth Hudson
OUR STATE GREATEST HITS **LEAD EDITOR:** Katie Schanze
EDITORS: Todd Dulaney, Katie Kane, Mark Kemp,
Katie King, Chloe Klingstedt, Katie Saintsing
DESIGN DIRECTOR: Claudia Royston
ART DIRECTOR: Jason Chenier
ASSISTANT ART DIRECTOR: Hannah Wright
EDITORIAL DESIGNER: Erin LaBree
ART ASSISTANT: Claire Audilet

Library of Congress Control Number: 2023909515

Our State
GREATEST
Hits
VOLUME I

We're joyfully revisiting some of the magazine's timeless and beloved features from the past decade. This selection represents a small snapshot of our state, from the places that call to us and the food we love to the Carolinians we admire and the memories we treasure.

WELCOME
A LOVE LETTER TO NORTH CAROLINA 4
Drew Perry

HOME SWEET HOME
CAST-IRON SKILLETS 10
Sheri Castle

ROCKING CHAIRS 12
Scott Huler

TELEPHONES 16
Susan Stafford Kelly

TASTE OF CAROLINA
SWEET TEA 20
Tommy Tomlinson

TOMATO SANDWICHES 24
Scott Huler

KEATON'S BARBECUE 28
Joe Posnanski

FRIED BOLOGNA SANDWICHES .. 34
Lynn Wells

PRIDE OF THE STATE
LINEMEN 36
Eleanor Spicer Rice

A PIONEERING PILOT 40
Mark Kemp

THE WOMAN WHO SAVED THE HORSES OF SHACKLEFORD BANKS 44
Jeremy Markovich

THE GREAT OUTDOORS
HEIRLOOM EARTH 48
Drew Perry

THE SCENT OF RAIN 52
Eleanor Spicer Rice

SNOW DAYS 54
Michael Parker

CAROLINA CRITTERS
FAMILY MULES 58
Robyn Yiğit Smith

DOGS OF WAR 62
Bryan Mims

PALMETTO BUGS 66
T. Edward Nickens

BORN & RAISED
GROWING UP CAROLINA 70
Susan Stafford Kelly

THE ROCK QUARRY 74
Mark Kemp

THE ACC TOURNAMENT 78
Adam Lucas

WATER SPICKETS 82
Susan Stafford Kelly

BELOVED PLACES
BOONE 84
Leigh Ann Henion

BALD HEAD ISLAND 88
Michael Kruse

MOUNT MITCHELL 92
Matt Crossman

APPEARED IN 2014

A Love Letter TO NORTH CAROLINA

Drew Perry has a crush on North Carolina, and he doesn't care who knows it.

ILLUSTRATIONS BY SUZANNE CABRERA

I've loved this state the whole time. I fell in love with it, though, at age 12, on a coed summer camp campout (impossible, that phrase; none of us could believe our good fortune), where I had my first kiss at an overlook — Eagle Rock — in the mountains outside Hendersonville. The night smelled like pine trees and rhododendron. Or hope and possibility. That was it, really — place and romance were, for me, twinned up forever.

Or maybe that wasn't my first kiss. Maybe my first kiss was plainer, in a fluorescently lit middle school hallway, but the summer camp kiss is the one I remember, or choose to. It came after dinner, after we'd hollered songs across the gorge to another camp, and they'd hollered back at us; after we'd sat up late in the dark, trying on some older age, telling each other things we were sure were true; after we'd headed to sleep, everybody sprawled, mostly chaperoned, under the same huge blue tarp. Then the kiss. Hurried. Clumsy. Fairly chaste. Then over. Then some intense hand-holding. We were 12.

A LOVE LETTER'S A MESSY THING. IT IS BY definition incomplete. You swoon, you forget, you leave things out. A love letter to a state is messier still, and it requires confessions: I've never been to the Outer Banks. I've only spent one night in Charlotte. The last time I was in Boone, I was in my 20s. I've never eaten a ramp.

A letter like this also requires infidelity, or something like it: If I talk about any one of the indie bookstores I haunt across the state (Malaprop's in Asheville, Scuppernong in Greensboro), then I'm shorting the dozens I must leave out. If I take pains to mention the way the land *finally* rises up across the border on Interstate 85 out of South Carolina, then I won't have space to talk about the tunnels on Interstate 40 just before you get to Tennessee. I'll probably have to name a beach. A hiking trail. There's a convenience store on my drive to work that's currently advertising LOCAL EGGS, DIABETIC SOCKS, and FISHING BATS. Surely a fishing bat is the best kind of bat, but that's not even the convenience store I want to talk about.

Maybe this is how it goes with love. It's not that we pick or choose. Not really. We just never have time to say it all.

A LOVE LETTER MUST START OVER, AND I want to start over in line, sipping a very cold honor-system beer, at Yacht Basin Provision Co. in Southport. I do love nearby Oak Island — love its not-quite-caught-up-to-last-week feel, its piers, its rental keys in paper envelopes, its houses nearly in the breakers, its fishmongers (I've found religion more than once over the grouper cheeks at Haag & Sons) — but I love lunch at the Provision Co. maybe most of all. Here's how it goes: You stand in line, a long line. You order. You eat — fish sandwich, onion rings, that sort of deal. On the way out, they ask what you had — they have no idea — and you pay. The whole thing runs

> **Maybe this is how it goes with love. It's not that we pick or choose. Not really. We just never have time to say it all.**

5

a sunny day in SOUTHPORT, NC

on the honor system, not just the beer. And I love this not for the chance to cheat, but to get up, pull a second icy bottle from the huge standing cooler, and return to my crab cakes without having to bother anyone to do it for me. There's a dock off the back of the restaurant, sound-side. Open-air. Boats trolling by. Fans on the ceiling, most with all their blades. Tiny paper napkins, nowhere near big enough to do anything. It's like eating at your house, if your house were much better, and at the beach, and full of fried food and good people. Or good food and fried people. Which I'm not saying it isn't, but still.

A LOVE LETTER WANTS TO TRY TO TELL THE truth, and the truth is that the finest sporting venue in this state or any other is Burlington Athletic Stadium, home of the short-season Rookie League Burlington Royals. A woman who's got season tickets behind the visiting dugout has, for as long as I can recall, sung "Green Acres" at the top of her lungs to the desperately bewildered opposing team during the sixth-inning changeover. There's an unidentifiable orange mascot that did not change over when the team switched from the Indians to the Royals. Right-center field has a dark spot on it. Some nights, hot dogs are a dollar. You can bring your lawn chairs and sit against the fence along the first-base line — for general-admission prices. If you want your baseball Disneyfied, then this isn't the place for you, but if you want it full of kids playing pickle behind the metal bleachers, if you want flashes of true talent between handfuls of walked-in runs, if you want that little pop-up tent beneath which last season there was an actual grill with actual hamburgers upon it — listen. I know, OK? I do. Minor league ball is minor league ball, but it is its own kind of heaven, no matter the home team. The Asheville Tourists. The Cape Fear Crocs. Ten other teams between them across this state. But with apologies to Durham and Crash Davis and Susan Sarandon and William Blake, my heart lies in Burlington.

I CRAVE THE LEAVES CHANGING OVER, A FIRE in the woodstove, a well-earned cup of coffee, a flannel shirt. I crave, then,

State Highway 21 from Elkin to Sparta, a kind of catchall smorgasbord of signs and signals that say you're no longer down in the flats, that you're headed for windows-open weather, for the High Country. A left-hand exit off U.S. Highway 421 lands you almost in another era, one of roadside motels, of flea markets, of half the businesses being named "State Road" this or that. There's a wooden sign directing folks toward an actual "Camp Cheerio." There are gas stations with flat-top grills, gas stations housing meat-and-threes, gas stations selling hand-spun milkshakes. All these gas stations also sell deer corn and blaze-orange stocking caps. There are Pepsi-Cola and Coca-Cola signs on the general stores. There are Cheerwine signs. Horse farms, cattle farms, Christmas tree farms. Twist your way toward the scenic overlook that aims back toward Grandfather Mountain, and then you're up and over the Eastern Continental Divide, past the Blue Ridge Parkway, and headed for Sparta, for the last decent grocery before you're nowhere, some cabin you've found, big back porch looking off into nothing, quiet nights, quiet mornings, boots and jeans and deer in the yard.

I'M DOING IT WRONG. I'M SMITTEN. Reeling. Counting the ways I love thee. Let's pull it together: Let's speak of the World's Largest Strawberry at The Berry Patch in Ellerbe — and of my son, age 3, standing atop a picnic table in front of said two-story strawberry, fists in the air, shrieking, and blazing through what remains of the largest sugar shock of his life, having eaten his entire ice cream cone and some of mine. I'm a sucker for the World's Whateverest Anything, but this place? I love the boulders in the lawn, painted, only half-explicably, like fruit. I love the road-weary families, sunstruck and confused about scale, wandering through the crushed-rock parking lot toward an open-air vegetable market and truly excellent ice cream. I love even the trash cans scattered around, housing sticky spoons and spent cups and legions of bees. The whole place may be an actual fever dream. Sitting out there in the long shadow of the fiberglass strawberry, it's almost hard to believe you're sitting out there. But you are, and what remains to be done is this: Clean your hands and face as best you can, try not to get stung, buy a few ears of sweet corn and maybe some tomatoes, crank up the AC in the car, and head on home.

BURLINGTON
ATHLETIC STADIUM
bottom of the seventh

7

AND HERE: LET'S ENGAGE IN A BIT OF ABJECT heresy. There's just no good way to love one barbecue joint more than another; there is no best barbecue in this state. That's the deal: To love North Carolina is to love each and every Speedy's or Jimmy's or Bubba's or Smiley's. Or: To love barbecue is to love North Carolina. I'm not going to stoop to East versus West, or ketchup versus vinegar. I'm instead going to lay down a few rules: The building should be cinder block or brick or corrugated metal. I humbly request a hand-crank hush puppy machine. We must begin and end with pork, though I will allow chicken or beef on down the menu. Slaw, in quantity. I enjoy a baked bean. There needs to be a counter bar as well as tables. Homemade sauce. Mugs sporting the name of the establishment, perhaps alongside a farm equipment advert or two. The über-classic Short Sugar's in Reidsville more than fits the bill here, but what I mean to say is this: To live and love in this state means to know where the barbecue is in your town, and where the place is within a couple of hours that's well worth the drive. Plus those spots in between. Plus that one place Down East. And the one from out near Hickory that time, however many years ago.

WE ARE IN NEED, FRIENDS, OF A STREET, a neighborhood — a place to call home even well after you leave — and that place is Carr Street, in College Hill, in Greensboro. The street itself is a block of tumbledown Victorians, graduate-student apartments jigsawed into the houses three and four at a time, a place of wildflowers and volunteer curbside cherry tomatoes and mint run amok and wisteria hanging off the phone poles. The place is about Jeff Towne, the kindest, warmest, absentee landlord I'll ever know, and Jim Clark, who runs the MFA program at UNCG, but who also, several times a year,

CARR STREET / COLLEGE HILL

ILLUSTRATION BY SUZANNE CABRERA

This state has all the geographies. Most of them, anyway. And each wants a love letter of its own.

discards his wrinkled suit jacket for torn denim shorts and a Hog's Breath T-shirt, which I can't believe still holds together, in order to grill ribs all day long. The smoke hangs like a beacon over the neighborhood, and past and current students and various hangers-on and several complete strangers show up by evening bearing sides, a kind of loaves-and-fishes deal that makes you believe fully in mac 'n' cheese, if not also the god of your choice. I learned on that street to fake being a grown-up. I learned what generosity looked like. I was again taught communion. I learned how to carve a slab of ribs on the tailgate of a pickup. Both my boys' first food was Jim Clark's barbecue sauce. You want to know the look of wonder? Feed an infant one of Jim Clark's ribs.

RIVERS NOT GETTING ENOUGH SPACE AND time here: the Haw, the New, the French Broad. Forests going wanting: Uwharrie, Nantahala. Dismal swamps not mentioned: the Great Dismal Swamp. Stone Mountain State Park near Roaring Gap will have to stand in for all of these, will, with its general store sitting down at the bottom of the hill, have to have front porch enough to rest up for every trail from mountains to sea. And it'll do fine. It's got a little something for everybody: family-friendly trails; less-family-friendly trails; trails with large signs warning, absent punctuation, 200 FT. FALLS AHEAD FATALITIES HAVE OCCURRED HERE USE EXTREME CAUTION. In our family, this makes for a ready-made Christmas card. In others, I suppose, it instills a somewhat more prudent fear. Still, to be in love in the here and now means to find somewhere to escape the interstates and Internets, to have some spot you know well nearby, to learn what weather looks like in a place that's not your own backyard, or the parking lot at Sears.

And now all this is turning hopeless. This state has all the geographies. Most of them, anyway. And each wants a love letter of its own.

You see? We've come to the end, and there's no chance to wax endlessly about the tamales and ceviche at Fiesta Grill in White Cross. There's no time to name the quiet campus spaces, like the quad in front of the glittering library at NC State, the old campus at Chapel Hill, the chapel at Duke, the shade beneath the Chinese fir off the northwest corner of Whitley Auditorium at Elon. I don't get to talk about the angry dog, circa 2005, biting the waves down on the wild south end of Topsail Beach, endlessly confused and each time expecting that *this* time the water would be fresh. I had some things to say about Highway 70, which runs from Hot Springs to Statesville to Kinston to New Bern. I did not mention the Appalachian Trail. I did not manage to name John Coltrane or The Avett Brothers or Doc Watson or Roberta Flack.

My first kiss was here. My first dog. I met my wife here, married her here. Had my first son. My second. A final confession: I'm not from here. Not originally. But I'm trying. I truly am. If you'll have me, North Carolina, just know that I've been yours all along. — *Drew Perry*

APPEARED IN 2017

CAST-IRON *Keepsake*

Many family heirlooms are too fragile to use often, if ever. A well-seasoned skillet is different. Everyday use enriches its flavor, and its story.

When cornbread is baked in a passed-down cast-iron skillet, every slice comes with a taste of the past.

The ancient Egyptians outfitted tombs with objects thought useful and necessary to the departed in the afterlife. *Hmmm.*

Perhaps I should ask my people to trundle me off to the sweet hereafter with my skillet by my side. You see, some people are born with a silver spoon in their mouths. I was born with a cast-iron skillet in my hand.

Cookbooks laud the culinary merits of cast-iron cooking, yet the power and persuasion of a good skillet is not what we make in it, but how using it makes us feel. If we're lucky, our skillet is a hardy heirloom, passed down with pride and imbued with stories that tether us to family tradition. A well-seasoned cast-iron skillet sports an ebony gleam that comes only from regular, heartfelt use. It's not a mirror, but you sure can see yourself in it.

CAST-IRON SKILLETS AND COOK POTS WERE a given in my family's kitchens, as certain and commonplace as knives, bowls, and aprons, but not all of those items were singled out as keepsakes. For something to be considered an heirloom, some sort of sentiment must develop. That happened for me when a beloved aunt died unexpectedly more than 30 years ago. I inherited her sapphire-and-diamond engagement ring and some of her cast-iron cookware. The ring is in a safe-deposit box, where I rarely see it. The pans are in my kitchen cabinets, where I use them almost daily.

Other family pieces bearing the hallmarks of Lodge, Griswold, and Wagner found their way into my heart over the years. My favorite is a nine-inch skillet that was handed down from my great-grandmother, named Lillie. To my knowledge, for upward of a century, nothing other than cornbread has ever been cooked in that one. (It is the plain truth that cornbread must be made in a cast-iron skillet.) Someday I will hand it to my daughter, named Lily.

I've also bought and refurbished old pieces from yard sales and flea markets, and invested in a few new items for my collection. Mercy, there's a lot of it, around 60 pieces. If you figure that each piece weighs about six pounds, that's around 360 pounds of sturdy iron. I doubt there was that much solid metal in my first car. And unlike my first car, my cast-iron cookware has never leaked oil, rusted through, or broken down. It works as well today as it ever did. Pound for pound, year after year, there's nothing else like it.

Most antiques need coddling and fussing over, but not a trusty old skillet. Yes, it warrants reasonable care, but if it were as vulnerable and fragile as people fear, we wouldn't have great-grandmother's skillet at all, much less be able to restore and perpetuate its original glory and utility. A cast-iron skillet is repeatable history.

The only thing that can wreck a good skillet is neglect and ambivalence. It asks only to be used regularly and well. In exchange, it will persevere for generations and do what it's meant to do: make meals and memories worth sharing.

If you aren't the current keeper of a family skillet, and possession isn't pending the reading of the will, then I am truly sorry about your lack of inheritance. But if you buy a good skillet to launch your own legacy (and make righteous cornbread), at least you'll have something to leave your children. It'll see you through in the here and now, and maybe in the great hereafter.

— *Sheri Castle*

APPEARED IN
2020

ODE TO A SOUTHERN *Rocker*

Finding the right chair for the front porch is an essential part of living the good life in North Carolina. But it takes time, patience, and maybe a failure or two.

I first learned that a rocking chair has a soul when I went looking for one. It was not long after I bought my home in Raleigh. The house had a small front porch, just big enough for a chair and a little table. A big-box store provided what you'd call a Carolina slat rocker: wood, with square rather than round spindles, and wooden slats for the seat and back. It had nice, wide armrests that turned out to be almost, but not quite, big enough to comfortably support a beverage — similar to the ones you see on the front porches of chain restaurants. I brought it home, primed it, painted it, and waited for it to dry. On the first pleasantly warm evening, I went out to the porch, drink in hand, and settled in.

And the rocker practically flung me back out. I happened to save the gin and tonic, but you may call that foreshadowing. The chair was poorly balanced, leaning forward just a bit too much. To sit comfortably, you

On the front porch of the historic **Mast Farm Inn** in **Valle Crucis**, kick back in a home-grown Bob Timberlake rocker.

PHOTOGRAPH BY REVIVAL CREATIVES

had to push back a little with your legs, which meant that instead of relaxation, the rocker caused tension. Yes, you could place your drink on its armrest, but the minute you tried to turn a page or adjust a cushion or — God forbid — rock, it was goodbye drink. I don't give up easily, though. I sat in that chair and spilled stuff. I tried to read, my calves getting tired as I hunched over my book like someone in a Rembrandt painting. As God is my witness, I played a banjo in that rocking chair! I did what I could. But the chair defeated me.

Still, that rocker was lovely to look at, painted a forest green to match the shutters. It sat on my porch aspirationally for at least five years, maybe 10. But as rain seeped in, the chair became wobbly. With so little reward, I was unwilling to maintain it, and I awoke one morning, finally, to *pieces* of a chair. The rocker and I parted ways.

THIS WAS NOT MY FIRST ROCKING CHAIR FAIL. I spent much of my childhood facing down a rocker that sat in the den of my family's brick house in suburban Cleveland. It had a broken back spindle that bedeviled me. Attached to a cracked socket at the top, the spindle would usually *sproing* away from the dowel that stuck down from the cresting rail. When the spindle wasn't wobbling back and forth, it was poorly glued — or duct-taped, or both — to the dowel, lending no support, but at least rendering its malfunctioning a little less obvious.

That broken spindle represented a moment, I was told many times, from my toddler-hood. My mother, sitting in the chair, had grabbed me for one of those rocking-chair hugs. I wriggled and resisted, refusing to cooperate. But for my mom, it was hug or bust, so bust it was, and she grappled with me until the spindle broke. My mom blamed toddler me; I cast no blame, but from then on, I avoided that chair. Looking back on it now, I think the poor rocker never had a chance. Once you're paying attention to it — once you're thinking about how it works, or even whether it's working — a rocking chair's heart is broken. The entire experience should be unconscious. You should be rocking in a rocking chair without even knowing it. Just as a rocking chair should not throw you out, nobody should wrestle you into a rocking chair.

A rocking chair isn't merely a piece of furniture; a rocking chair is a contract.

You find yourself in a rocking chair. Because a rocking chair isn't merely a piece of furniture; a rocking chair represents a contract. Between chair and person, between seat and seated. The rocking chair is a way of saying, *Let's be here now, for this moment.* Or maybe not exactly here: here-ish. We're not pushing, we're not pulling, we're just going back and forth a bit, and we're not thinking much about it. A rocking chair, in fact, is even more than a contract: It's a statement of beliefs about the purpose of a chair, about the structure of a day. A rocking chair is a meditation on the nature of sitting down.

THERE ARE MILLIONS OF COMFORTABLE chairs, but a rocker has that other level: It quite literally moves you. I've gone through many rockers in my life, from the one that I broke while resisting my mom to the one that rotted on my porch to the ones that my wife and I inherited from our grandmothers, which turned out to be not quite right. I've thought about it, and, for me, what a rocker needs is a combination of the things that my failed rocker relationships lacked.

First, as I learned from my porch rocker, it needs to comfortably rock. A good rocker should lean backward on its own. It should beckon you to, as it were, sit in its lap. When you sit, it should embrace you, not pitch you back out. And second, it should comfortably hold you — and, all right, maybe also an infant or a compliant toddler — but usually only you. If you want motion while you canoodle, sit on a glider or a porch swing. A rocker is more of a driver's seat. There's no space for a passenger, so don't try to cram one in. Something will break.

And that kind of tension is what the rocking chair is meant to avoid. Sitting down to make a shopping list? You have a kitchen table for that. Need to discuss things with the kids or your spouse? There's the living room couch. But sitting down just to sit? That's what your rocking chair is for. We think of retirees rocking on porches because relaxation, lack of obligation, is what a rocker represents. It moves back and forth, but it doesn't *go* anywhere. You can toss in every Southern cliché you like — tea, liquor, shade, seersucker — and a rocker improves each one. A rocking chair is the paprika of furniture: It intensifies.

The rocker must rock not so much with you as *for* you; you should be rocking without even knowing that you're rocking. If someone complains about a noise you're making as you sway back and forth, unaware that you're rocking? That's a good sign. If you're humming and you didn't notice? Another positive. Researchers have found that rockers induce the kind

The rocking chairs on the front porch of the Durham-Davis House in Wilmington are like time machines, gently transporting sitters back to the late 1800s, when this Queen Anne-style Victorian was built.

of brainwaves you experience just before sleep. Not for nothing did my mom want to rock me when I was a toddler. Who is ever done with rocking their children? But, as my mom learned, it's also important to make sure those children still want to be rocked. They may have reached the age of wanting to rock on their own.

After our misses with our inherited rocking chairs, my wife now sets up shop in a rocker that came from an abandoned house, reupholstered and loitering in a corner of our dining room. She reads there, listens to podcasts, and is slowly, gently, digging a hole in the drywall with one of the runners. I pointed it out to her once, and she looked up.

"Oh," she said. "Was I rocking?"

Good job, rocking chair. — *Scott Huler*

Telephones were a girl's best friend in 1954. Southern Bell operators (picture dated 1939) connected the party group to select boys — and sometimes parents listened in on the party line.

APPEARED IN
2014

PARTY ON THE *Line*

Telephone operators once helped connect folks across the state before "If you'd like to make a call ... " became standard.

For three minutes only, and only on a Sunday, only between noon and 5 p.m., or after 7 but before 9, and only station-to-station, not person-to-person, and never ever collect unless you have an emergency (though it felt so wonderfully important to be able to say, "Collect").

Admit it. Remembering today's passwords and PINs is child's play compared with memorizing rate information to make the least expensive telephone call, known until only recently, by the way, as long distance. Plenty of people remember when our pocket-size telephones were larger than shoeboxes. Even the accoutrements were wondrous: When I wasn't turning over the clever miniature hourglass — three minutes! — beside my grandmother's phone, I was continually flipping the alphabetical tabs on the spring-up early Rolodex of frequently dialed numbers next to it.

In 1879, three years after Alexander Graham Bell commanded Thomas Watson to "Come here, I need you," telephones arrived in North Carolina, and the first long-distance call was made from Raleigh to Wilmington on April 14. Another three years, and Southern Bell opened in Raleigh with 24-hour service via two operators and — imagine! — 29 "subscribers." Southern Bell had also begun or purchased operations in Greensboro (1889), Wilmington (1890), Winston-Salem (1891), and Asheville (1899). Meanwhile, Down East, G.A. Holderness and other businessmen established an exchange in Tarboro in 1895 with a capacity of 50 lines in Washington, Kinston, and Fayetteville. By 1900, Carolina Telephone and Telegraph Company (CT&T) had operators in Maxton, Smithfield, and neighboring towns serving 1,645 customers. By 1927, nearly every town in eastern North Carolina had telephone service. The combined impact of these two providers was drastic: immeasurable, unimaginable, and, as we have seen, unstoppable.

Previously, a barn fire, a burst appendix, or a rolled tractor on a family farm often equaled death and destruction as the family watched helplessly. Every older person I spoke with (over the phone, naturally) mentioned that in that era, if you were fortunate to have a telephone, you shared it.

IN THE 1930s, THE 1,100 RESIDENTS OF WALNUT Cove relied entirely on Miss Birchy and her switchboard. Never mind a formal office; the switchboard was in her house. As my mother walked home from school, Miss Birchy might come to her front door and holler, "Your mama said to tell you she was runnin' into Winston!"

In Wayne County, Dr. Hank Stephenson's family phone was the standing version made familiar in movies, with a mouthpiece, a long barrel, and a side hook for the receiver, but no dial. "Number, please," answered the operator, known by everyone as "central." When Stephenson's elderly mother moved to Little Washington, she announced that, "Y'all have the meanest central!" because the robotic female voice so often broke into her (mis)dials, relentlessly repeating, "That number is no longer listed. Please check and try again."

Take it from Margaret Adams: Meanness was not permitted. Adams began work as an operator January 7, 1949, at Greensboro's only Southern Bell office, on Eugene Street. Adams was an information operator, local operator (when there were only four for all of Greensboro), toll — or long distance — operator. Whether on a split shift, night shift, or day shift, Adams sat under the

The purpose of telephones hasn't changed over the years — they still connect us around the world and to our loved ones.

watchful eye of a supervisor, who perched on an elevated chair "to make sure we didn't misbehave."

Lauch Faircloth, 86, remembers driving seven miles to Clinton to make telephone calls. The switchboard was located in a room over Reynolds Drugs. "You'd tell Mamie who you wanted to call, she'd connect you, and you went into the booth located in the same room to talk," the former senator says.

How many smiles and sobs, questions and confessions have traveled the swaybacked lines?

"The operators knew everything and didn't mind telling it. I remember precisely when we got a phone at home. November 1941. One Sunday we came home from church and the phone rang. It was the sheriff calling my father to tell him Pearl Harbor had been bombed."

UNFORTUNATELY, NO ONE IS ALIVE TO RECALL the earliest days of telephone service in North Carolina. The party-line stories, however, are alive, well, and legion if you nudge them. With their distinctive rings — one for the Smiths, two rings for the Joneses, three for the McGillicuddys — party lines had nothing to do with dancing and socializing, but with the number of families, or "parties," sharing the same line. Except, of course, when they did have to do with parties. As a child in Wrightsville Beach in the 1960s, Katie Redhead spent rainy days eavesdropping on Mrs. Lehto chatting to Mrs. Broughton about what they were wearing to the Surf Club, and what would be on the menu.

A friend from Oxford reminds me that the one phone families had was always in a reverent location. But in 1958, CT&T introduced the first colorful telephones, in a Kinston motel, and the telephone became a consumer object. Reverence waned and crank calls ensued. *Do you have Prince Albert in a can? Why don't you let him out?*

Weekdays at boarding school, we were allowed to use the phone only between 9 and 10 p.m. All day you'd fondle your quarters to feed the phone to talk to your boyfriend, constrained by the ticking seconds, the glares of impatient classmates, and that terrifying blankness when the machine was calculating, gurgling your coins, deciding whether to grant an additional three minutes with your beloved, or to cut you, and your budding romance, off.

Thank you, Southern Bell and Carolina Telephone. Thank you for permitting a state of textile towns, wee hamlets, and family farms, stretching from mountains to sea, to be knit together. Thank you for helping to save lives, and time, and comfort homesick children. Thank you for the delivery of news — joyous, tragic, or trivial. Thank you for this marvel, this — tool? gadget? machine? — instrument we so blatantly take for granted.

How many smiles and sobs, entreaties and apologies, questions and confessions, answers and demands, proposals and denials, and of course, memories, have traveled the swaybacked lines I watched on car trips, lulled by that dip and rise, undulating and unending and dependable? Most of us would rather return to the days of horse and buggy than relinquish our telephones. Communication always trumps travel.

And speaking of traveling ... *Is your refrigerator running? You better go catch it!*

Click. — *Susan Stafford Kelly*

APPEARED IN
2010

Sweet CAROLINA

In our dining rooms and diners, we stir together a handful of humble ingredients to produce an amber elixir that tastes like the South and feels like home.

"OK, this is how we make the sweet tea," Anita Hall says.

Anita has waited tables for at least 25 years here at Pressley Park, a meat-and-three a few miles south of Uptown Charlotte. She shows up at 3:45 a.m. to brew tea for the cops and construction workers who want breakfast before dawn, and the families who take home jugs for the weekend, and the guy from Baltimore who picks up two gallons every time he goes home so he has something to drink with his crab cakes. This tea is the color of a baseball glove, but clear enough to see through. And in one cold glass you taste the South — the sweetness of a hunk of cane sugar, the tannins of a black-water creek.

The joke at Pressley Park is that Anita doesn't drink the tea — she likes coffee better. But every morning she starts making tea, and by closing time at 3 p.m., they'll have gone through 35 to 40 gallons.

"So you take this" — a five-gallon container — "and put the tea in and fill it halfway with hot water," Anita says. "Then stir in the sugar. Then put in more water. Then we put in a little ..." And all of a sudden, three voices holler, "No!"

One belongs to George Gregory, who runs Pressley Park. The others belong to his dad and mom, Andy and Tina, who opened the restaurant and still help out. It turns out there's a secret something in the sweet tea. They'll laugh when you try to figure it out, but they aren't about to give the secret up.

The truth is that there's a secret something in every glass of good sweet tea. You can doll it up if you have a mind to, but all you really need are tea bags and sugar and water. Somehow, though, when you put them together, it's magic.

Brewing tea like Pressley Park's Anita Hall is sure to lead to a sweet smile on someone's face before long.

PEOPLE DIVIDE THE SOUTH FROM THE NORTH at the Mason-Dixon Line, but I've always thought the real marker is the sweet-tea line — the point where, at the next diner north, they don't have sweet tea ready to pour. I'm not sure just where the line is. I feel sorry for those poor souls up above it. But one thing's for sure: North Carolina is on the good side.

And over the years, in this part of the world, sweet tea has become infused with meaning. It's more than just a drink. Sweet tea is our alchemy — our gift of making something special from humble ingredients. (Just like barbecue, conjured into glory from the cheapest cuts of meat.) Sweet tea is our love offering, poured for family and neighbors and even the guy trying to sell us new gutters. And at its most basic, sweet tea is a cold blast on a hot day, like a dip in a river from the inside out.

We have been drinking sweet tea down here for nearly two centuries now, although the tea of the early 1800s doesn't much resemble what most of us drink with cornbread and greens. Back then, the tea was green tea, and it was served as an ingredient in punch — spiked with champagne or rum, and sweetened with sugar and cream.

By the early 20th century, most people in the South drank black tea imported from China or India. (All types of tea come from the same species of tea plant, *Camellia sinensis*; the different types of tea come from different varieties or how the leaves are processed.) Cookbooks had recipes for basic sweet tea, but people still drank it mostly in punches. The two big events that converted the South to the sweet tea we know today were Prohibition, which got rid of (most of) the nation's alcohol, and ice delivery, which gave people a way to cool down a big glass. By the 1930s, sweet iced tea was as common at the Carolina table as salt and pepper shakers.

YOU CAN BUY SWEET TEA ALL OVER THE country now, way past the sweet-tea line. McDonald's sells it nationwide. Just about any convenience store sells a bottled or canned version; you can even find it in vending machines. But if you're in North Carolina, and you buy sweet tea in a can ... well, bless your heart. Maybe you could just hide it in a paper bag. What we're talking about, when we talk about sweet tea, is something brewed that morning, stirred by hand, served by a waitress who calls you darlin', poured out of one of those special pitchers with the spout on the side, or better yet, sitting in the fridge at your mama's house.

Deet Gilbert teaches about tea as part of her Essentials of Dining Services class at Johnson & Wales University in Charlotte. Part of her job is to help future restaurant managers understand the economics of tea — it's so cheap to make that sometimes the ice in the glass costs more. (Even with free refills, tea is one of the biggest profit-makers on the menu.) But she also wants her students to understand the culture of tea, all over the world, and especially in the South. "Those tea punches, back in the 1800s, were made for social events," she says. "And I think that tradition has continued, even though tea has also become something you'd just normally have at the table. A glass of tea is the first thing you bring out when you have a guest in the house. It's the connection you make with someone to make them feel welcome."

Sweet tea is homemade. And it's part of how you make your home.

Even within the simple sweet-tea trinity — tea bags, sugar, water — there are all kinds of variations. Some people steep the tea for half an hour, some let it sit all day. Some people throw in a couple extra bags to boost the astringency — the thing that makes your mouth a little dry, like a glass of red wine. And then there's the sugar. "I know some places you feel like you better have a good dentist before you drink the tea," Gilbert says.

That's true — every so often, you'll take a swig of tea that would be better off poured over pancakes.

But this is part of what makes sweet tea so intoxicating. It's homemade, if by "home" you mean all those little Formica diners and smoke-smudged barbecue joints scattered across North Carolina like pepper flakes. One day, the tea guy's not paying attention and dumps in too much sugar. Or your sister's making it at home and ends up one bag short. Or you're off up North somewhere, trying to turn Lipton's finest and tap water from a glacier lake into something that reminds you of a summer night in Wilkesboro. Sweet tea is homemade. And it's part of how you make your home.

ANDY AND TINA GREGORY, THE FOLKS AT Pressley Park, put a lot of work into their sweet tea. They arrived in Charlotte 30-some years ago from Greece, after a brief stop in Boston. When they opened their first restaurant, the House of Pizza, they didn't know how to make sweet tea. But every day they brewed a pot, and every day they asked their customers how it could be better. After a few weeks, nobody complained anymore.

They say they haven't changed the formula since — and that goes for the secret ingredient, too. It's great sweet tea. But the truth is, it tastes a little different every day — depending on how hot the water is, and how many strokes Anita Hall takes when she stirs the sugar in, and what time of day you order it. There's no magic formula, because sweet tea is about people. That's the magic part. — *Tommy Tomlinson*

PRESSLEY PARK
740 Pressley Road
Charlotte, NC 28217
(704) 525-9393

Who can complain about the heat when summer makes such delicious sandwiches possible?

APPEARED IN
2011

Southern HEIRLOOMS

The classic tomato sandwich's roots may reach beyond the Mason-Dixon line, but there's something about this summer staple that gives it a special home in our kitchens.

What I am going to say may cause some discomfort. But I urge you to hear me out, for in the end I bring a message of joy.

I hope you won't begrudge my first premise, which is that Southerners, proud of a regional culture with roots as deep as the red clay, have something of a propensity to claim things. It's hard to deny this, right? Whether it's porches or storytelling, acoustic music or the land itself, Southerners take pride in not only their traditions, but also the contributions of those traditions to the culture at large — and can even, on occasion, stretch those contributions a tad. Southerners can be especially proprietary about food. Whether it's grits or okra or collard greens or hard-boiled eggs or anything else on an almost numberless list, Southerners say it belongs, somehow, exclusively to the South. Which makes it perhaps all the more an affront that I must, after thoroughly researching the topic, make the following statement: The tomato sandwich is not a Southern food.

Yes, I know: the tomato sandwich. Two pieces of white bread: Merita, say, or Wonder; maybe Bunny, if you're from Tennessee. Duke's mayonnaise — and only Duke's mayonnaise, about which more later. A thick slice of tomato, dripping oozy goodness. A little salt and pepper, if you like.

WHAT I'M SAYING IS THAT IT'S NOT A Southern thing at all, that tomato sandwich. As my own community-supported agriculture farmer Tom Kumpf says, "That's not a Southern classic. That's a summer classic." Kumpf lives — and grows tomatoes, among other crops — on his Double T Farm in Garner, south of Raleigh. In fact, the tomato is why Kumpf's farm exists. "What really got me going in the garden was wanting to eat my own tomatoes," he says. And who can blame him? A fresh-picked tomato, still radiating the sunshine that grew it? That's heaven on earth.

Kumpf sent me to Craig LeHoullier, the Raleigh tomato maven whose website, NCTomatoman.com, casts a long shadow on the North Carolina heirloom tomato landscape. Among his accomplishments is the popularization of the highly sandwich-friendly Cherokee purple tomato, famed for the nice meatiness that holds a tomato sandwich together. He lived all over the country, and he prefers his tomatoes in slices on grilled cheese sandwiches.

Whatever else goes on a sandwich, LeHoullier says, "the tomato is critical." As an heirloom tomato guy, he strongly believes a good sandwich needs an heirloom tomato. "You go to the farmers market," he says, of hybrid tomatoes, "and you see piles of the big, red, perfectly round ones. If you tossed them at someone with any kind of speed, you'd probably injure them for life." The favorite heirlooms of the Carolinas, both Kumpf and LeHoullier say, are the Cherokee purple and the German Johnson, a North Carolina native cultivar that's a great big beefsteak, which basically means it slices well.

LeHoullier also has no loyalty to the store-bought white bread of the classic sandwich, preferring a nice ciabatta or farm bread. And then he utters the greatest apostasy of all. "I don't eat mayonnaise," he says. "I've probably never eaten what is called the great Southern tomato sandwich."

That sandwich, if it exists, has Duke's mayonnaise on it. "On both sides," says Erin Corning, Duke's associate brand manager. "Because if it's not dripping down your chin while you're eating it over the sink, it doesn't count."

The tomato sandwich is Duke's signature recipe. Bread, tomato, mayonnaise. Corning can (and does) go into significant detail about mayonnaise ingredients. Duke's gets its tartness by using no sugar, for example. Kumpf and LeHoullier, too, talk for hours about things like the balance of acid and sweet in a tomato.

"If it's not dripping down your chin while you're eating it over the sink, it doesn't count."

But as for ingredients, if you're looking past tomato, mayonnaise, bread, you're overthinking the tomato sandwich. For even there, as good as Duke's mayonnaise is, I am not prepared to yield that a local type of mayonnaise stakes an entire sandwich to a region, or that putting a piece of mozzarella or some basil on it renders it somehow inauthentic. I watched my mother make her tomato sandwiches with Miracle Whip (she tells me she's switched to Hellmann's now) in northeastern Ohio; you make them with Duke's on your Carolina front porch. How does that make the tomato sandwich a Southern food? It's like the South claiming bread, or the clothesline, or elbows. True, where would we be without them, but it seems to me the Union soldiers probably appreciated them as much as the boys in gray.

Craig LeHoullier is known for popularizing the Cherokee Purple tomato — the East Tennessee variety that inspired a deliciously colorful heirloom tomato boom.

SO MY POINT COULD NOT BE MORE thoroughly made: The tomato sandwich is a summer, not a Southern, food. It belongs to the world, not the South. My conclusion is simple, well supported, and straightforward.

So, of course, cue backpedaling.

Once I had drawn my conclusions, I did what I usually do and sat down to discuss them with my wife, June Spence. Raleigh native, lover of food and all good things, June spoke about tomatoes and tomato sandwiches in a way that was, for lack of a better word, Southern. She gave the same recipe as everyone else: Duke's mayonnaise, a thick slice of tomato, and white bread. "I don't think it's Southern," she says. "It's just what you get when you've got a lot of people growing tomatoes in their gardens."

Like in … the South?

"My grandmother just had rows and rows of them," June went on. Her grandmother lived in Angier. "As soon as they were ripe and as long as the plants lasted, there would always be a windowsill-full. And you'd always get sent home with them."

And one more thing. Maybe up North, where you've got lots of Italian immigrants and a shorter growing season, you could cook tomatoes down and save them as sauce. Not June's grandmothers: "I don't remember either of them canning tomatoes, which you can do. But you don't cook a fresh tomato," she says. "A fresh tomato is meant to be eaten raw."

Perhaps on … you get the idea.

So, a homegrown crop with a long growing season, consumed by people used to doing for themselves, and a sandwich that's a quick and convenient way to eat it. With a native condiment that somehow makes it special. Maybe the tomato sandwich, Southern style, *does* have a claim to iconic status. In fact, maybe that tomato sandwich and I have a few things in common. Like me, the tomato showed up here in the South as an immigrant — and stayed. In fact, it's gone all over the world, but somehow it seems to have found a special place for itself here, prospered, made a home.

Which describes the modern South right down to the kudzu, yes? A place of simple things with long stories, where immigrants bring new ingredients and make them work, changing them but leaving them still somehow themselves, perhaps even more themselves for the newness.

Maybe we say this: The tomato sandwich is as Southern as … as Southern as … as Southern as anything else. — *Scott Huler*

PHOTOGRAPH BY TIM ROBISON

27

APPEARED IN 2017

THE MAN.
THE DIP.
THE *Legend.*

B.W. Keaton got people's attention when he started serving barbecue-sauced fried chicken at his restaurant in Rowan County. People are still talking, and the first question is always the same: How do I find this place?

With a bottle of Keaton's Famous BBQ Sauce, you can make the best homemade, dipped fried chicken your family has ever eaten. Almost as good as what they serve at Keaton's. Almost.

Burette Walker Keaton, founder of Keaton's Barbecue

"If you want to be entertained, go to a club. We're here to feed you."

— Robert Keaton, brother of B.W. Keaton

By all accounts, B.W. Keaton was a man uninterested in compromise. If you wanted to try his glorious fried chicken, dipped in his secret-recipe barbecue sauce, you had to earn it. You had to find his cinder-block restaurant in the middle of nowhere. You had to hope it was open — B.W. Keaton wasn't much for keeping consistent hours of operation. You had to wait, sometimes for hours, and hope they didn't run out before you got to the front.

If you were lucky enough to get some of that chicken, there were only a few booths and a counter to eat at; Keaton's didn't have a full dining room until B.W. died in 1989 and his niece Kathleen Murray added one after she took over the business.

And if things ever got a bit too rowdy, well, everyone knew that B.W. Keaton kept a shotgun underneath the checkout counter.

That, friends, is what real fried chicken is all about. We have moved into a time where so-called fried chicken is everywhere — on sandwiches and in buckets, cut up into tenders and nuggets, pushed on us ceaselessly by semiliterate cows who try to distract a burger-loving nation. The thing we call fried chicken now has become ordinary, a Happy Meal, a six-pack, something to snack on until a more exotic option comes along.

But fried chicken — real fried chicken — is the food of the gods. It's the best food ever invented for connecting people, for gatherings with family, for reunions and picnics and Fourth of July get-togethers and after-church socials. It is the only food, other than perhaps pie, that is equally wonderful hot and cold. And it is, unquestionably, the best food for conversation. People open up over fried chicken like they do for no other food.

Yes, I suppose that as a writer for a reputable magazine I should have some support for this conversation theory, some scientific or statistical evidence that proves or at least suggests that fried chicken is better for conversation than, say, spaghetti and meatballs or barbecued ribs or chili or anything else. I do not have such evidence.

But if you want, we can meet at Keaton's and talk about it.

THERE ARE TWO BASIC CHALLENGES WHEN IT comes to partaking in the religious experience of eating the fried chicken at Keaton's Barbecue. First, there's getting there. Keaton's is technically in Cleveland, North Carolina, which is technically in the middle of nowhere. B.W. Keaton grew up in a farmhouse down the road, and he started selling chicken in a shack nearby after he got laid off from the railroad in 1953. He had various offers through the years to build a full-service restaurant in Statesville or even Charlotte; he would sooner have sold his barbecue sauce recipe to the devil.

Actually, it wasn't the devil but the Schlitz Brewing Company that at one point tried to buy Keaton's barbecue recipe. The offer, as legend goes, was $10,000. Keaton told Schlitz to get back to him when they got to $100,000.

So, Keaton's has not moved and won't move — if you want to taste Keaton's hot dipped fried chicken, you have to hit the road. To get there, you drive to Statesville, then you take one of the exits, and then you drive until you're lost. And then you're there. If you stop along the way to ask for directions, the person will tell you: "Yeah, just keep going, you're just not lost enough."

When and if you get to Keaton's, you will know it by the "Keaton's Original Barbecue" sign out front. It has one of my all-time favorite slogans: Best by taste test … "Real Goood."

I'M NOT SURE WHAT TASTE TEST WAS EVER actually given at Keaton's — I suspect B.W. Keaton would have pulled out the shotgun if anyone ever suggested one — nor do I know to whom to attribute that quote, "Real Goood." I imagine it is a direct quote from every single person who ever went there.

The second Keaton's challenge is getting to the restaurant when it's open. B.W. Keaton opened the place more or less when he felt like it. This tradition has endured. The hours of operation at Keaton's make for a poem that someone might want to crochet:

Keaton's BBQ
Is closed on Sundays and Mondays
On Tuesdays it is open from 11 to 2
On Wednesdays it is open from 11 to 2
and 5 to 7
Or 7:30

B.W.'s secrets are in good hands: His niece Kathleen Murray has run Keaton's since 1991.

On Thursdays it is open from 11 to 2 and 5 to 7
Or 7:30
On Fridays it is open from 11 to 2 and 5 to 7
But not 7:30
And on Saturdays it is open from 11 to 2 and 5 to 7
Or 7:30
All hours are subject to change
You can call this number for reservations
But Keaton's doesn't take reservations
The take-out menus at Keaton's and the sign out front actually have its hours listed as 5 to 8 from Wednesday to Saturday, and when I ask the woman behind the counter about the discrepancy, she explains by saying, "Yeah." The spirit of B.W. Keaton insists that if you want the wonder of Keaton's Barbecue chicken, you have to work for it.

IF YOU GO TO THE KEATON'S WEBSITE — oh, what would B.W. Keaton have thought about a website? — you'll come upon a real treasure: a video piece on Keaton's recorded by Carolina Camera. It features an interview with B.W. Keaton himself. Well, it's not exactly an interview — he doesn't actually stop cooking to talk — but he says a few words:

TV reporter: "What's in that sauce, B.W.?"

B.W. Keaton: "A lot of things."

He does share the inspiration for his sauce.

"An old man about 92 years old and myself got together, kind of like a football huddle," he says. "And that's what we came out with. It'll penetrate the chicken. Then penetrate the bone."

> **B.W. Keaton didn't believe in giving out any utensils. You have your fingers, don't you?**

He wasn't lying. This chicken is fried and then dipped right into that magical barbecue sauce. You should know that when and if you get inside Keaton's, you will have several options: In addition to the choice between white meat and dark meat, you can order a half chicken or a whole chicken. And ... no, that's pretty much it. You do have the option of ordering the chicken hot or mild, though you should be warned: When I ask the woman behind the counter about the mild, she offers a look of such deep disapproval that I feel like I have publicly shamed my entire family.

That sauce is pretty hot on first taste, but then, magical as it is, your body acclimates to its wonder. That sauce does penetrate the chicken, the bone, your lungs, and your heart in more ways than one. It's impossibly delicious. They tell you that it also prevents the chicken from being greasy. It probably cures a host of ailments and various diseases, too.

There are side dishes at Keaton's, which are fine and are extra and are beside the point. When you order the chicken, you get the chicken ... and a white bread bun. You also get a plastic fork and knife, which might not sound like much, but it's a new thing. B.W. Keaton didn't believe in giving out any utensils. You have your fingers, don't you?

There are all sorts of signs with rules inside Keaton's. No weapons are allowed. No swearing is allowed. You can use a credit card if your order is more than $5, but if you are using cash, you must pay with exact change in small bills. And, you are not allowed to take photographs of the employees. It's not entirely clear what necessitated that rule.

But you work through all of it because this is real fried chicken, the sort that was fried for special occasions in black and white households in the South going back hundreds of years, the sort of fried chicken that inspired people to go seeking, the sort of fried chicken that inspired people to buy cars in the first place.

On the day I make it to Keaton's, two friends join me, and of course we have the greatest conversation about a million things because that's what real fried chicken does. We talk about music and love and food and wonder. Yes, B.W. Keaton's brother had it right. You bring your own entertainment to Keaton's. They provide the chicken.

— *Joe Posnanski*

KEATON'S BARBECUE
17365 Cool Springs Road
Cleveland, NC 27013
(704) 278-3048
keatonsoriginalbbq.com

APPEARED IN 2022

LUNCH BOX *Love*

A childhood spent eating homemade sandwiches for lunch and a husband with an affinity for bologna inspired a Greensboro chef to test her culinary boundaries with a familiar ingredient.

Rockford General Store in Surry County is known for its fried bologna creations — topped with hoop cheese or chili and slaw for a Carolina-style treat.

The best fried bologna sandwich I've ever made was an accident. The deli attendant at the grocery store cut the meat much thicker than I'd asked for, but fried bologna is one of my husband Chip's favorite sandwiches, so I decided that I'd surprise him with a grand concoction.

When you order a fried bologna sandwich at a general store or lunch counter, fry cooks often make half-inch cuts around the edges of the slice to keep it from curling when it's cooked. This slice was so thick, I didn't even have to cut it.

I heated the cast-iron skillet until it was almost smoking and placed the bologna onto the scalding surface. When fatty meat with that many spices hits a hot skillet, the aroma is divine. After about a minute, I turned down the heat and flipped over the bologna. After another minute or two, a perfect char formed a border around the slice. I toasted two slices of rye bread — Chip's favorite — and topped each one with Duke's mayonnaise and American cheese. I also might have added a thick slice of a Cherokee Purple tomato from Stan Beam's farm in Cherryville. I plated the monstrous sandwich, put it in front of my husband, and waited for his reaction. He couldn't contain his surprise: With more expression than I've seen in years, he said, "Good Lord! Now that's a bologna sandwich!"

We'd both grown up with bologna sandwiches, but nothing *that* fancy. My own introduction to bologna was in the lunchroom at Claxton Elementary School in Greensboro. I often bought lunch from the cafeteria, but on special days, Mom would send me to school with a homemade meal. She always bought Oscar Mayer bologna — I remember the yellow-and-red package with red bands around each slice — and either Wonder Bread or Merita. Her recipe is a classic: two slices of fresh white bread, two or three slices of bologna, a slice or two of American cheese, and yellow mustard (Duke's optional). While I was in class, the thermos of cold juice inside my metal lunch box kept the sandwich cool until the bell rang and I took my seat in the cafeteria.

Meanwhile, Chip's mom, Nancy Wells, a Monroe native and schoolteacher, made sandwiches frequently for her two growing boys. Every summer, the whole family would head down to Carteret County, where the boys would fish in the surf at Harkers Island and explore the seafood scenes in Atlantic Beach and Morehead City. Just after our wedding in 1986, I got a taste of Chip's childhood summers at the Crystal Coast. We joined his parents on their annual vacation to The Atlantis Lodge in Pine Knoll Shores as a sort of honeymoon. Nancy and I read on the beach while the men fished, as Chip had done as a kid. At lunch, Nancy prepared the sandwiches he'd loved growing up. Pimento cheese and bologna with bread-and-butter pickles on white bread; turkey, ham, Swiss, tomato, pickles, and pickled okra on rye; and a Wells family staple — roll-ups made of thick-sliced bologna stuffed with cottage cheese or whatever else was on hand. My husband couldn't have been happier to taste bologna at the beach again.

As a personal chef, I spend my days creating and customizing menus and recipes for my clients. I can't say that I've ever gotten a request for a bologna sandwich in my years as a private chef — at least, not from the people I cook for whom I don't live with. On the weekends, I enjoy experimenting with different flavors folded into my finds from the farmers markets in Greensboro and, occasionally, happy accidents from the deli counter. But I know that Chip would be just as happy having a simple bologna sandwich. I'll make both with love.

— *Lynn Wells*

Between the end of the 19th century and the middle of the 20th, linemen worked to bring North Carolina into the light.

KEEPERS OF THE *Light*

It's easy to take for granted the gifts of electric heat and light, but it wasn't so long ago that much of our state lay in darkness. Our thanks to the workers who faced — and continue to face — sleepless nights, dizzying heights, and the constant peril of electrocution to give us power through the simple act of flipping a switch.

Scott Faulkner dangles atop a 40-foot pole overlooking Mount Airy. A slender leather strap figure-eights around him, one loop around his bulky frame, one loop around the wooden pole. Metal spikes "no bigger than ink pens" jut from his boots, tiny cat's claws keeping him from a four-story tumble. Death coils around him like a silent, invisible snake, but Faulkner is nimble, skilled, and he knows how to avoid it. He also knows that many like him have not been so lucky.

Faulkner is not a thrill-seeker. He is a line-crew foreman, and this is his job.

Electricity pools around him in a transformer, shoots through lines zigging and zagging from Mount Airy outward in all directions, illuminating, powering, rolling, whirring through our homes, across our streets, and into our stores and factories. To understand Faulkner and the power he tames and gives, we need first to go back more than 120 years, when North Carolina was in the dark.

IN THE EARLY 1880s, THE WORLD HAD ELECtric fever. Thomas Edison's bright light bulb first flashed in 1879 but, like most new technology, was years from working in homes. Instead, large cities like London and Paris replaced the gas lamps that lined their streets with arc lights that snapped a bow

By 1970, nearly every home in North Carolina had power, making transformers a common sight.

of electricity between two electrodes.

In 1881, the Arista Cotton Mill in Salem (now Winston-Salem) flipped on North Carolina's first electric lights. The arc lights ran off a generator, helped workers avoid accidents and work longer hours, and ignited a fascination with electric lights that soon spread to Raleigh, Charlotte, and New Bern's city streets. By 1888, North Carolina's urbanites could stroll safely after dark. To save money, many cities shut off the lights on full-moon nights.

The demand for lighting grew. Power companies like Thomson-Houston Electric Light Company began popping up like fireflies in summer, using "dynamos" to convert mechanical energy to electricity and selling it to cities.

City dwellers petitioned for well-lit homes, and power companies happily recognized the untapped profit. They hired linemen to erect light poles and connect power lines between poles and residences. Ground men, or "grunts," ran materials to the linemen from the ground.

With little understanding of this emerging technology and no safety procedures in place, the work was dangerous. Murray Walker, cofounder of the International Lineman's Museum in Shelby, says that the linemen's high pay could not compensate for their dangerous work. "One out of every two linemen died from 1880 until the early 1900s," he says.

We made our own starlight, threw it into the night sky, from cities to the edge of habitation.

Meanwhile, to bolster the public's need for electricity, power companies sold appliances, touting simplification of residential chores like laundry and cooking. Before long, city dwellers couldn't imagine life without the ease power provided. But rural areas still went to bed when the sun went down.

UNTIL THE 1930s IN NORTH CAROLINA, ONLY urbanites enjoyed electricity. Profit-driven electric companies saw little incentive to power rural areas.

In 1935, President Franklin D. Roosevelt

established the Rural Electrification Authority (REA) to help farmers power their land. During the next 20 years, linemen laid tracks for many North Carolinians to see electric light for the first time.

BY THE 1960s, NEARLY EVERY HOME IN NORTH Carolina was illuminated. We made our own starlight. We threw it into the night sky, from cities to the edges of habitation.

Picture the night sky — can you? Are you picturing the sky you really see at night, the sky you remember, or a sky you've seen on an electrical device? Do you see the soft orange or green hue glowing into the darkness from your city or town?

Although our state's central nervous system of power courses through our towns, the linemen's work is far from over — and far from safe. Today, linemen rig power to new construction and bandage the old. All the while, electricity surrounds them. Current is quick, silent, odorless, invisible, and lethal. It seeks ground and takes the most direct path to get there, from trees to roots, fingers to feet, through hearts or livers, muscles and ligaments. It scorches those who touch it from the inside out, a deadly streak through the body's system, sometimes causing deep burns, sometimes killing.

Even today, with safety standards and new technology that insulates and protects, like rubber hoses, blankets, gloves, and sleeves, the job remains perilous, among the top 10 most dangerous jobs in the United States.

Often the unnoticed first responders to disasters, linemen sometimes leave their families in the dark so they can power others' homes. When we're left in darkness after an ice storm or a hurricane like Fran, it might be difficult to see the people who drive through the night across treacherous landscapes to bring us power again. But they're there, harnessing and distributing volts, helping restore our lives.

"Sometimes I have to leave my family in the cold to go put others' lights on," says Faulkner. "But if you make a line hot in the middle of the night and see everybody's lights come on? That's a good feeling. You say, 'At least they're going to be comfortable for tonight.'"

POWER ITSELF HAS CHANGED ACROSS North Carolina. What once pulsed only on a heartbeat of coal or water's rush now also throbs to the thump of splitting atoms at nuclear plants like Shearon Harris in New Hill, or blazes to the ancient energy of the sun at solar farms across the state. The jump and snap of arc lights now glow cool with halogen or LED. And although life without power makes for a nice weekend adventure, many of us would be left in more than the dark, with no way to acquire gas for our cars, no hospital access, no credit cards.

For now, Scott Faulkner and his linemen peers are still responsible for illuminating towns across our state, providing the power we don't see until we miss it. Today, Faulkner sees another kind of power pushing open the day. He sways on his pole in Mount Airy and watches the sun peek above the horizon.

"Up there on the pole, all of a sudden it hits you; all of a sudden it's daylight, and you can see what you're doing without your headlamp on," he says. "You look out across the ridge and the sun coming up over it. It makes you kind of warm-feeling, you know? You're doing something that matters; plus, you get to see a lot of sunrises."

Here, even while strapped to the present, we can still unplug.

— *Eleanor Spicer Rice*

APPEARED IN
2021

Freedom AT 20,000 FEET

A young man's love of open spaces inspired him to start his own airline, blaze a trail into history, and pass his knowledge on to a new generation of pilots.

The old man was not formally educated, but 10-year-old Warren Wheeler hung on to his every word during those summer days in the bright glare of sunshine on rippling water. The old man was a waterman, and young Wheeler his student. The child had learned plenty from his own highly educated father, the president of the Mechanics and Farmers Bank of Durham, who would later help draft the Civil Rights Act of 1964. Wheeler also learned a lot from his mother, a Howard University and Hampton Institute graduate who long served as the head librarian at what was then

PHOTOGRAPHY BY ALEX BOERNER

40

Wheeler is a familiar sight on the tarmac at Person County Airport, but he's more at home in the skies above it.

known as the Durham Colored Library. But this old fisherman, Charlie Harris, taught Wheeler things that his parents couldn't.

Harris regularly invited the kid on excursions into the open water, where Wheeler learned what freedom felt like. But freedom can be fleeting. The Coast Guard eventually told the old waterman that he had to be certified before he could carry people out in a boat. And being certified meant passing a test. "Well, he couldn't do that because he couldn't even read or write," says Wheeler, who, many years later, would found the nation's first Black-owned air carrier, Wheeler Airlines. "But there was nobody I'd rather be out in the water with than that man," Wheeler continues, "because he knew more about the water than anybody."

One day, Harris let Wheeler take the steering wheel. When Wheeler turned too sharply, cables got wrapped around the wheel, and the boat went into a spin. The fisherman remained calm. He "quietly, calmly came up, took my hands off the steering wheel, and straightened everything out," Wheeler says. "And he looked at me, and he says, 'Son, don't mess with what you don't understand.'" Wheeler, now 77, laughs as he recalls the valuable lesson. "If that's not an educated man, we don't understand the meaning of the word education."

WHEELER WAS 3 YEARS OLD THE FIRST TIME his family packed up their car and drove from their home in Durham to the peaceful Robert R. Moton House in Gloucester, Virginia. It was the earliest of many annual family trips to the stately brick mansion that butts up against the blue-gray waters of the York River. Wheeler grew up longing for those summer escapes, where he came into contact not just with modest fishermen like Harris, but also with prominent Black leaders who were ushering in a new era of freedom in the 1950s.

Wheeler balanced piloting 737s for Piedmont Airlines (left, 1976) with flying his own fleet of aircraft for Wheeler Airlines (right, 1977).

Inside the Moton House, legal minds hashed out strategies for cases that were part of the Brown v Board of Education ruling, which rendered school segregation illegal in 1954. And it's said that the Rev. Dr. Martin Luther King Jr. put the finishing touches on his 1963 "I Have a Dream" speech while relaxing on a stone bench under a tree outside. The Moton House was a think tank and a vacation spot for wealthy and influential African American movers and shakers to take their families during a time when Black people of all social and economic strata were barred from white resorts and conference centers.

For young Wheeler, though, freedom wasn't just the new advances in civil rights that he was hearing about; it also meant looking out over the sprawling York River, or up into the vastness of a cloudless Southern sky. When he returned home to Durham, Wheeler would think back on the conversations that he'd heard around the Moton House table — like the time the president of Tuskegee Institute described what it felt like to fly an airplane upside down. "I would be like, *What is he talking about?*" Wheeler says incredulously. *"How do you get an airplane to fly upside down?* Black people didn't even fly in little airplanes back then."

The image stuck with Wheeler, and when his older sister, Julia, who was taking flying lessons, was invited by an aircraft salesman for a short trip in a little four-seat Cessna 172, her younger brother tagged along. Before then, Wheeler had dreamed of sailing boats in the ocean — now, he dreamed of piloting airplanes in the wild blue yonder. "After that flight," he says, "I was hooked on airplanes."

Wheeler once dreamed of sailing boats — now, he dreamed of piloting airplanes.

Wheeler was just 16 when he earned his private pilot's license. Two years later, he enrolled at the Agricultural and Technical College of North Carolina (now NC A&T State University), but soon grew bored with his classes and dropped out to study aviation at the American Flyers School in Ardmore, Oklahoma. At 19, after graduating from the AFS program and earning his commercial pilot's license, Wheeler set up shop in Chapel Hill, where he began teaching white college students from the University of North Carolina how to fly.

In the early 1960s, getting work as a pilot for a major airline was next to impossible for a young Black man. Wheeler applied for jobs, but no one was calling back. Meanwhile, he earned his flying hours by accompanying a pilot who flew charters and by continuing to teach flying lessons. He applied for a job at Piedmont Airlines and didn't hear back after the interview. Luckily, his father was friends with Gov. Terry Sanford, who had flown on some of the charter trips that Wheeler copiloted. Sanford knew Piedmont Airlines' president, Tom Davis, and made a call on Wheeler's behalf.

In 1966, Wheeler became Piedmont's first Black pilot and, at 22, one of its youngest. He continued his flight school in Chapel Hill, and in 1969, while still flying for Piedmont, he launched Wheeler Flying Service, a cargo and courier operation, and eventually its commuter and charter wing, Wheeler Airlines.

AS WHEELER'S LITTLE AIRLINE GREW, HE WAS burning the candle at both ends, piloting for Piedmont, heading his own company, and encouraging his employees to all chip in on duties. By 1976, the company that Wheeler had started with just two Piper six-passenger planes and one employee — himself — had a fleet of 11 planes and 27 employees. He'd expanded his reach across the state, and his revenues averaged more than $20,000 a month. Most of his passengers were white businessmen, many of whom worked for the Durham-based Burroughs Wellcome pharmaceutical company and would travel back and forth between Durham and the company's factory in Greenville. The rest of his business consisted of cargo and courier contracts with companies ranging from banks to the U.S. Postal Service.

Wheeler Airlines remained the only minority-owned airline in the nation until the early '80s. Shutting down the airline in 1986 was a hard decision for Wheeler, but it turned out to be fortuitous. "Now I can help kids get into it," Wheeler says, "and that's much more of a contribution."

Part of Wheeler's mission all along was to train and employ more Black pilots. By 1978, seven of his 14 pilots were Black, and two copilots were women, one of whom was a Black woman. Breaking color and gender barriers and encouraging other aspiring pilots of color is "Warren's platform for history," says Anita Neville, who works for Wheeler's current nonprofit, Airolina Young Aviators of Durham. Airolina is an aviation STEM (science, technology, engineering, and math) program that's available to all teens, but its focus is on underserved Black and Hispanic students. "He's retired now from any commercial work," Neville says, "but his goal — and it's our model at Airolina — is to pass it on."

DURING THE HEIGHT OF HIS CAREER AS PRESident of Wheeler Airlines, Wheeler kept a 22-foot sailboat in Norfolk, where he'd escape to on free days to decompress and reflect on his childhood experiences boating and fishing with his mentor, Charlie Harris. In more recent years, Wheeler has kept a 32-foot sailboat docked in the Caribbean, where he's continued to seek the freedom that he felt while gliding across the sun-speckled waters of the Chesapeake Bay. Whether he's sailing across the water or soaring 20,000 feet in the air, the experience — being alone, surrounded by nothing but deep, deep blue — is pure, and he's free.

— *Mark Kemp*

APPEARED IN 2016

THE
Survivors
OF SHACKLEFORD BANKS

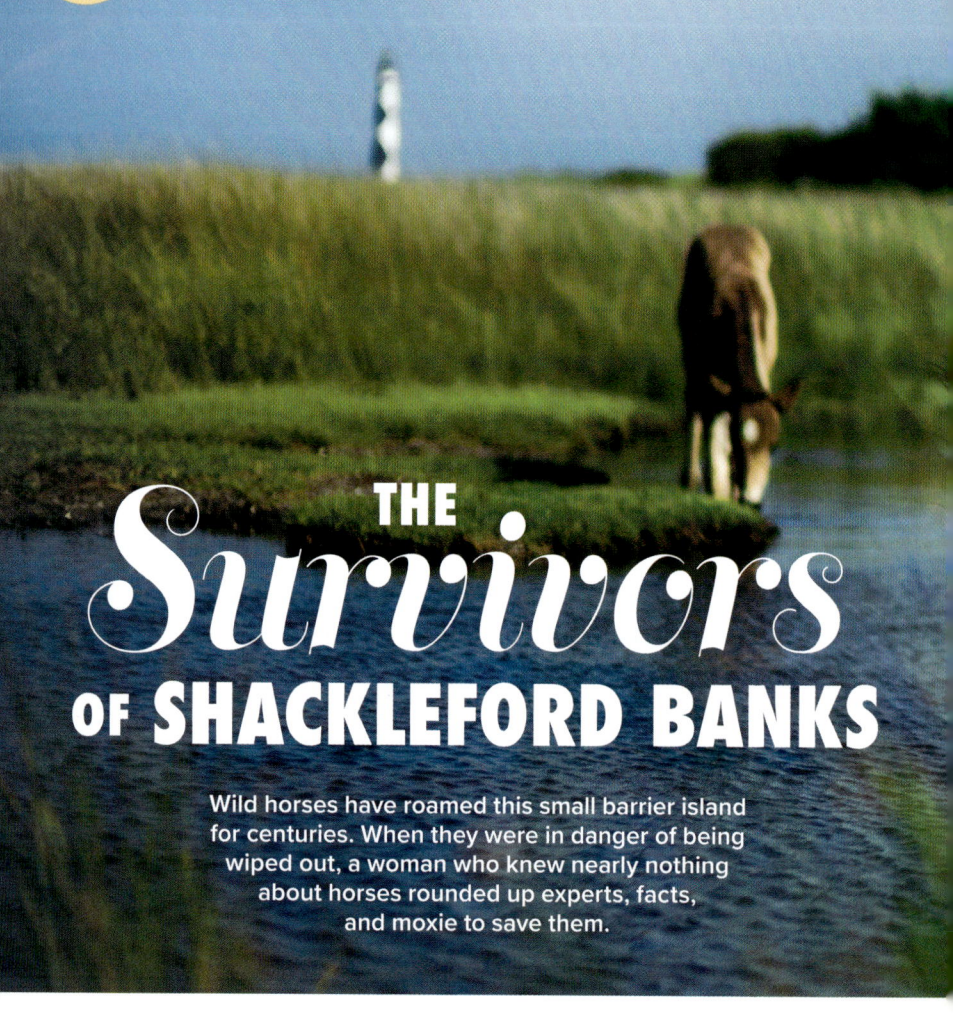

Wild horses have roamed this small barrier island for centuries. When they were in danger of being wiped out, a woman who knew nearly nothing about horses rounded up experts, facts, and moxie to save them.

As the pontoon boat ferry approaches the east end of Shackleford Banks, the young, floppy-haired captain spots some horses standing on the muddy shore. He slows the boat, and dozens of sightseers in swim trunks and sun hats turn their heads to look.

The captain gets on the loudspeaker to throw out a few loose facts. "These horses," he says, "don't get medical attention."

"That's not true," Carolyn Mason says under her breath. She doesn't raise her voice. She doesn't make a scene. For years, she's been correcting misconceptions about

PHOTOGRAPH BY CHARLES HARRIS

44

By law, the number of wild horses on Shackleford Banks ranges from 120 to 130, which is considered the ideal number for a healthy herd.

the horses on Shackleford.

When the ferry stops on the sandy tip of the island, across a channel of blue water from the Cape Lookout Lighthouse, several people with towels and coolers clamber off, heading toward the wider beach on the south side of the banks. Carolyn heads north. She hugs the shoreline, slogging through the mud and salty streams.

Carolyn wants to get a close look at a foal that's just a few weeks old. After 10 minutes of walking, she spots it and the rest of the herd. They're eating green spartina grass, their favorite meal on the island. They're also on the other side of a tidal creek. The water's rising, and it's already too deep to cross. Carolyn stares for a few minutes, hoping that the horses will cross in the shallows so she can get a better picture of the baby. But they barely move.

"You can't be in a hurry over here," she says, sighing. "They're not."

Carolyn decides to check on some of the other horses she knows. Although she rarely needs it, she has a photo album at home with glossy pictures of each horse, identified by a system of letters and numbers.

CAROLYN WALKS UP A SMALL DUNE SPARSELY covered in grass and heads toward the blue Atlantic on the south side of the island, covering the constant climbs and descents with ease for a 72-year-old. In the valleys, mosquitoes and flies buzz around, so she's wearing long sleeves and pants on a hot day.

This place, a nine-mile-long barrier island between Beaufort and Harkers Island, has always been harsh. Once, a town of 500 people stood on the flatter, eastern end, but the last person moved away three years after the 1899 hurricane. In the years afterward, fishing shacks and ramshackle cottages, meant for weekend getaways for locals, popped up. Cows, goats, and sheep grazed here. The horses were rounded up from time to time. When President Lyndon B. Johnson signed a bill establishing the Cape Lookout National Seashore in 1966, the days were numbered for the shacks and livestock, both of which were gradually removed. And for a time, it looked like the horses would be, too. That's when Carolyn got involved.

She quickly deflects praise, but everyone, from nationwide experts to colleagues and friends, says that without her, a free-ranging population of these horses would no longer exist. "Carolyn's the mover and shaker who made that happen," says Dr. Daniel Rubenstein, a professor and prominent equine biologist at Princeton University. "Don't let anyone tell you otherwise."

AS SHE CRESTS A DUNE, CAROLYN SPOTS TWO young horses, a stallion and a mare. Carolyn takes notes to pass on to a ranger. Carolyn has years' worth of horse stories to tell. Once, she saw a horse drinking out of a salty tidal creek at high tide. That can't be, she thought, because the horses only drink from fresh springs, or from small, snout-size watering holes dug out with their hooves. After the horse left, Carolyn waded out to the exact spot where it had been drinking, and took a sip. There was a spring directly beneath her feet, and the water was fresh. The horse knew.

When the odds are against them, they forget how small they are.

It's hard to believe that 25 years ago, Carolyn knew little about horses. She'd only seen them a handful of times, mostly on Shackleford. She'd grown up along the water in tiny Marshallberg, which lay underneath the sweep of the Cape Lookout light. When she returned to the area to continue her career as a base librarian at Marine Corps Air Station Cherry Point in nearby Havelock, she got involved only because a coworker asked her one day if she was going to "the horse meeting" in Beaufort.

This was 1995, and Carolyn and others were horrified by what they heard. After the National Park Service removed the livestock, the horses had no competition for the grass on the island, and their population doubled. The horses were technically feral: They had been introduced to the island by man, which made them a nonnative species. If they ate too much grass, the park service was concerned that erosion might endanger the whole island. As such, the park service considered the horses pests.

After the initial meeting, Carolyn learned that 76 Shackleford horses had contracted a contagious equine disease called equine infectious anemia, and would be euthanized per state regulations. She and others protested, but couldn't stop it. They were further worried that if the population kept dropping, the herd would slowly fade away. Carolyn and a handful of others began forming the Foundation for Shackleford Horses, and went to work to save the rest of the horses. Because Carolyn was a librarian, the new nonprofit decided she should be in charge of rounding up facts. She emailed congressmen using a dial-up connection at her home, and cold-called professors from a stool in her kitchen. Soon, she was able to get genetic testing done on the horses to prove the old stories that had been floating around Beaufort for generations: The horses really did come from 16th-century Spanish galleons that had shipwrecked or whose sailors had thrown the animals overboard.

Eventually, Carolyn got the attention of U.S. Representative Walter B. Jones Jr., who, in 1997, introduced legislation to protect the Shackleford horses. Senator Jesse Helms pushed it through the Senate, and a third North Carolinian, White House Chief of Staff Erskine Bowles, convinced President Clinton to sign it. One day, the NPS considered the horses pests. The next, the agency had to consider them protected.

More than 20 years after she got involved, Carolyn is still busy, still

Carolyn Mason led the campaign to protect the wild Shackleford horses. Without her, they may have disappeared.

observing, still learning, and still helping the horses. Over the years, she's learned something remarkable: Put a wild horse in with a larger domesticated one, and nearly every time, the wild horse will become dominant. When the odds are against them, they forget how small they are.

AFTER FIVE HOURS OF TRUDGING ACROSS dunes in the hot sun, Carolyn has given up on getting a closer look at the new foal, when suddenly, the horses she's been looking for appear. Fuzzy and a little unsure of itself, the foal wobbles a bit on its new legs. "Come on," Carolyn says softly, "let's see your face." The foal looks over for a fleeting moment, Carolyn gets a picture for her album, and then she and the herd walk off in opposite directions, if only for now.

—Jeremy Markovich

Heirloom EARTH

Letting kids discover what's beyond those breakers, past that bend in the trail — there, just out of reach — requires trust and faith, and yields the stewards of tomorrow.

The Appalachian Trail offers splashes of beauty in spring. On Roan Bald, between Round Bald and Grassy Ridge, a patch of New England groundsel blooms.

APPEARED IN
2018

We took you because we wanted you to see, to hear, to feel. To jump off that boulder in the North Fork of the French Broad and then stare back at us, eyes wide and full of shocked, frigid knowledge. To climb aboard a seaplane, for real life, as one of you said, and imagine what it would be like to look down at the land sliding past, at the rivers meeting the sea. To open a train window or stand on the deck of a ferry and put your hands — or your faces — into the wind.

We needed you to feel lost, to be lost with us. To follow the blazes until we couldn't quite follow them any longer, to trust first the old dog and then the new dog to help us find our way back. To trust a dog. To understand what it is to hike along a ridgeline that's not quite dangerous, not really, but where it matters that you pay attention all the same. To hike to a bald where we could look down at the hawks and buzzards circling below. To catch hold of the notion that, soon enough, all of this might belong to you.

The writer and his wife, Tita Ramirez, show their young sons the most beautiful spots in North Carolina, including Mingo Falls in Cherokee.

PHOTOGRAPH BY NICK BURCHELL

We took you to state lines to teach you about here and there, about boundaries and demarcations and the names we try to put to things. We took you to state fairs to teach you about rides and fried food and the wobbly feeling of riding back home along a dusky interstate, the headlights of oncoming cars blinking through the median. We took you to museums and libraries to show you — prove to you — that there was quiet in the world. We took you back home so you could show us that there wasn't, not really, not until you fell asleep. My God, how we loved bedtime. You both slept, each of you, like you'd fallen from some great height. Most nights, you had.

> **We wanted you, most of all, to remember. To understand what *inheritance* means.**

We took you to the edge of the ocean and lied, promised you'd be safe, that everything would be fine. What was it that you two named the water past the first set of breakers? Barely Scary. *Can we go out to Barely Scary?* And each year we did, in a raft I spent an hour blowing up, just like my own dad did for me — the inescapable, asphyxiating ritual of fatherhood. Out we went in that damn raft, and we only tipped a few times, enough times to teach you the difference between in the boat and not, enough times to teach me the difference between fun and fear.

We stood in the waves and helped you surf, helped as much as we could, told you the trick was just to believe you could do it, on your knees first and then standing, as though anything were that simple. We let the waves roll you, send you under, and when we needed to, we lifted you, sputtering, back above the surface. That green-black feeling of not knowing which way is up, salt in your nose, heart hammering — *that* we couldn't teach you. We had to let you find that, and find what to do with it, by yourselves.

We took you to fields and cut you loose. We showed you bats and lightning bugs. Taught you how to look for Orion — *Hey, Daddy, it's that guy!* We tried to show you truly dark night skies. We let you climb trees, let you climb far higher than we should have. You taught yourselves to ride bikes, paddle kayaks. We sat at the edge of a dock on some mountain lake and fought about whether we were letting you paddle too far. *I can swim out there if there's a problem*, I told your mother. *Not in time*, she said — which was right, of course.

We let you go, we let you go, we learned to *try* to let you go. Only a little at first: around the bend in the trail, up the beach a ways. Into the woods. Around the block on your bikes. Down the big hill on the sled — by yourselves. We traveled with a first aid kit and needed it all the time, congratulated ourselves over cocktails for letting you get far enough into trouble to require taping and bandaging.

We hoped, I guess, that we might raise you to do the same — to take your own dogs and kids, if you want them, out into the world. To wash their wounds. To teach them, in turn, to take care and become familiar. We wanted you, most of all, to remember. To understand what *inheritance* means. How to live here, in this place, this heirloom earth. To know — to really know — what it means to say you're from somewhere, and what it means to call a place home. — *Drew Perry*

APPEARED IN 2018

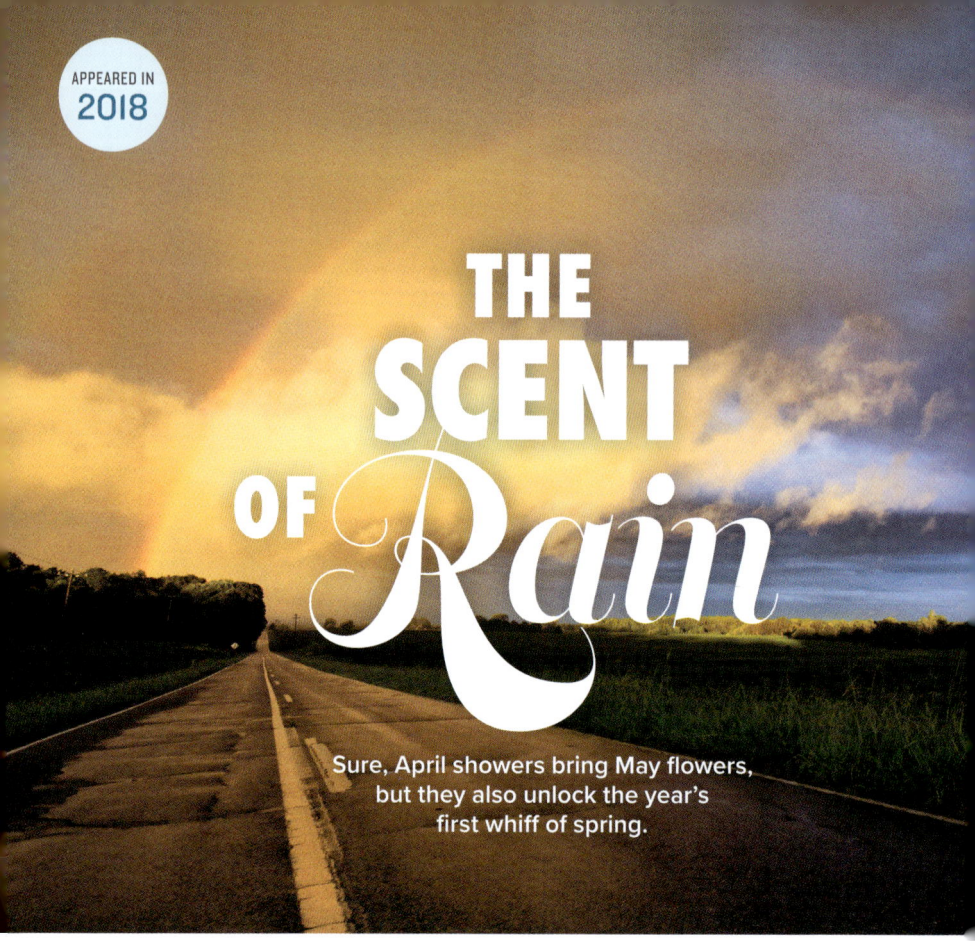

THE SCENT OF *Rain*

Sure, April showers bring May flowers, but they also unlock the year's first whiff of spring.

Petrichor, the smell of rain, comes softly but suddenly, almost like an idea. It rises from the cracks of city sidewalks, the damp straw floors of pine savannas, the blades of grass in suburban yards. It talks to you, tells you it's just fine to slow down a minute, to roll over and tuck back in, because it's going to be a while.

When we smell rain, we're not smelling actual raindrops. Instead, we're smelling the natural world talking to itself. Between rains, as the earth dries, tiny bacteria turn to dust within it. Plants release oils into the ground around them, sending their seeds a message:

"It's not safe to grow now. The ground isn't ready. Wait a little longer, if you can."

But then it rains.

When it rains, those oils, the silent advice of plants and the last gasps of bacteria, rise from the muddying ground and fill the air. That's petrichor. Or at least *technically*, that's petrichor.

Scientists captured petrichor in vials, ran it through complicated machines, labeled every molecule. They spied on it, took videos as it swelled and rose from the earth. They came to the conclusion that you came to as a child: Petrichor is sublime. It's a relief.

After a heavy thunderstorm in Iredell County, an empty stretch of Ingram Road north of Statesville blooms with the smell of petrichor.

It is a smell, with feeling.

The word marries the Greek word *petros*, or stone, with "ichor," the blood that flows through the veins of gods. The union of the ordinary and the divine. The grounding and ascending. The primordial understanding that raindrops on dry ground have always been a necessary step to begin righting living things.

Other scents mingle with rain. The gentle almost-there of azaleas around our front porches, the steamy asphalt of city streets, the metallic iron of red clay, the green whispers of leaves, warm bricks, rocks — the building blocks of our homes, streets, memories. No rainstorm, and no place in the rain, smells exactly the same. Because of that, sometimes the rain comes and simply calms. Other times, it kicks up a breath of gardenia and zoysia grass, or the wet wood and peeling paint of damp windowsills, and we remember.

The rain recalls those times as children when the most important thing to do was to press our faces to the screen door and watch the thump and splat of a cautiously budding world. To count the *plinks* on windowpanes and roofs and to have the time to wait them out. Without knowing it, we listened to the plants. We waited just a while.

Some say we've felt grateful for the smell of rain since we were scratching charcoal animals on our caves' walls. They say it calms us because it reaches deep into our cells, to memories before our own, when we understood that rain brings sustenance. It brings out the rabbit, the deer, the ripening berries, the reaching tubers. It brings cleansing, not with human soap and human hands, but with the natural way that life takes care of itself. So we listen to the advice of plants, hunker down, wait just a little while for the world to come forth. We feel life tremble, like the seeds underground, patient and ready. We wait for the signal, that rock and ichor, those kisses and long, easy afternoons, to give us permission to come 'round.

Now is the season. The lush, verdant world is returning. The sap rises, the creatures begin to pip night songs beneath the leaves, and we wake feeling rested and ready, our bundled winter beds and dark mornings a cold memory. Now's the time when it's just warm enough that we, getting out of our cars one afternoon or walking to get the paper one morning, smell the first petrichor of the spring.

— *Eleanor Spicer Rice*

APPEARED IN 2015

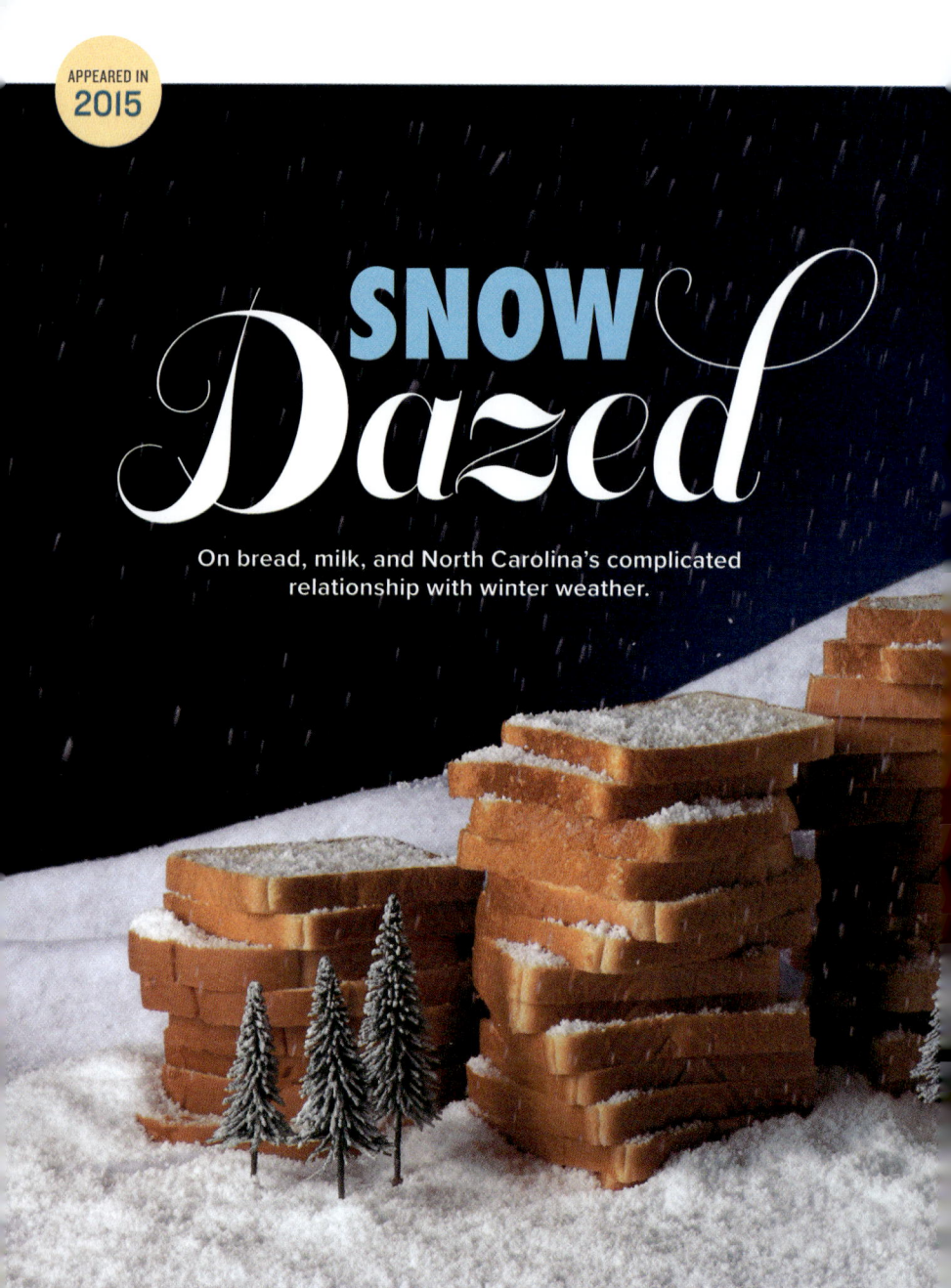

SNOW Dazed

On bread, milk, and North Carolina's complicated relationship with winter weather.

PHOTOGRAPH BY: MATT HULSMAN

55

We were having a wintry weather event in the Piedmont Triad, by which I mean four or five snowflakes had been spotted in the median of I-40 between Winston-Salem and Burlington. The highway patrol had been called out to wave along the rubberneckers trying to catch the first glimpse of precipitation. Part-time baggers and checkers had been called in on their day off to man the aisles of the local Harris Teeter, which was quickly running out of bread, milk, batteries, candles, and beer.

I was just settling in at home — classes at the college where I teach having been canceled for the week — when my friend Stuart called me up and asked me to turn on the television. Just like a Yankee, I thought. Of course I already had the television on, and the radio, too. Regularly scheduled programs were being interrupted for the latest news of the impending storm. The oldies station had faded out "The Lion Sleeps Tonight" mid-*wimba-way* to bring us the latest on road conditions.

My television has *been* on, I said. Stuart told me to tune in to the local news. As if I were sitting around watching the soaps. Stuart, see, was born and raised in Atlantic City, New Jersey. He went to college in northern Ohio, graduate school in Iowa, and had moved to Greensboro after a decade in Boston. He had told me stories about Iowa winters during which he did not wash his hair in the morning for fear of it icing up on his way to class. I had a hard time picturing this not only because it was so exotic to me, but also because I had to imagine Stuart with hair.

What? I asked. I was starting to get annoyed. I might have been missing the Doppler.

Don't you see him? Stuart asked.

A weatherman bundled up in an oversize, fur-lined parka stood in the parking lot outside the station. In one hand he held a saltshaker and in the other an ice cube. He poured some salt on the ice cube to show us just exactly how those noisy trucks turned the roads from ice to slush.

The local weathermen turn into cheerleaders, working us all into a frenzy.

Can you *believe* this? Stuart asked. Having once searched for an hour for his car on a Boston side street after it had been buried beneath a drift, only the tip of its radio antenna visible, Stuart found this demonstration wildly funny. To me, however, it was riveting, the information it imparted valuable. It might seem dramatic to a transplant, but high drama is just as much a part of what we call "some weather" as leaving work early in order to avoid getting stuck with only a quart of skim milk. During such an event, the local weathermen turn into cheerleaders, working us all into a frenzy. You can almost feel their pulses quickening from your sectional sofa as you sip hot chocolate and bank the fire. Six to 10 inches! Don't drive unless it's an emergency! Black ice!

It doesn't matter that, more often than not, our weathermen are either premature or inaccurate in their predictions. It's hardly their fault if a storm takes a turn. Either way, we get a couple of snow days and a month's supply of bath tissue out of it. Plus, there are times when the prediction is conservative, and we get walloped. A few years ago, I was dating a woman who had moved back to her hometown in North Dakota. It was February and 20 below in Fargo. I sold her on some 60-degree sunny days. Get on down here; we'll lay out, I said. (I had to explain to her what "lay out" meant, but once she got it, she was packing her sunscreen.) She landed on a tarmac barely swept of the snow that had been falling for eight hours. Although our blizzard was but a dusting to her, she was not pleased with me, having packed only sandals, a light sweater, and some Coppertone in her featherweight carry-on.

Those of us who have lived in the state for a while are fond of reminiscing about those pre-global warming days when the state got some *serious* snowstorms. I left the Coastal Plain for college in Boone just in time for the winter of 1978. My dorm was at the top of a vast parking lot down which we slid each morning on ice so thick that four-wheel drive was useless. For weeks, we threw snowballs and snow-themed parties.

Then there was the infamous March storm of 1993. It was my first year in Greensboro, and I'd decided to pull my 3-year-old daughter down to the park on a sled when the wind picked up and the socked-in sky flashed with lightning. Lightning during a snowstorm? Say what? My daughter was impressed, but I slipped a half-dozen times in my bulky work boots running that sled up the hill, terrified that we would freeze to death a half-block from the house and not be discovered until the azaleas bloomed.

Pretty to look at, but I'd just as soon not mess with it, we say when the snow arrives. Tons of sand and salt to make roads safely navigable are not a big line item in our municipal budgets. I'd be willing to bet that most towns in the state allot more money for Fourth of July fireworks than for overtime pay for snowplow drivers. Lots of people who have relocated here to *get away* from snow are puzzled, if not put out, by what they see as our lack of preparedness. But unlike more northerly climes, where piles of exhaust-blackened snow hang around the curbs from November to April, our wintry weather does not linger. Even though schools may stay closed for a few days due to patches of ice on rural roads, the day after brings only the constant dripping of thaw, the gurgle of snowmelt draining into storm gutters. Occasionally, a particularly hardy snowman survives for a week or so, a soggy toboggan on its head, a baby carrot for a nose. A photo of this shrinking survivor might crop up on the front page of the newspaper, a reminder of how wildly we anticipated that quiet blanket of whiteness, and how happy we were to see it go.

— *Michael Parker*

STUBBORN *Love*

Pulling a heavy load of history, mules were once considered family — at least, until tractors came along. But in certain quarters, our long-eared, hardheaded friends never went out of style.

In a small pine forest in the shadow of Research Triangle Park's sleek temples of innovation, four mules lie buried in an unmarked cemetery. The graveyard isn't easy to find, even with GPS coordinates. But part of the magic is stumbling through briars and thickets and happening upon their hidden chapel in the woods. There, among the twisty Carolina jessamine vines, are the sturdy granite tombstones engraved clear as day: "Maud. Brown mule. Very gentle," "Kate. Steel gray mule. Very intelligent," "Lulu. Bay mule. Very sweet," "Rose. Black mule. Very good."

No doubt some long-gone farmer's higgledy-piggledy expression of devotion: Lulu in the middle, Rose over there. Maud is buried a little to the right. Kate's nearby. It's easy to imagine their tails swatting flies off each other's backs. They lived between 1902 and 1946, and here, less than a mile from the nearest Starbucks, they'll rest for however many decades to come.

Growing up, it was important in my family to know something of mules. My grandfather's stories about plowing fields and riding mule wagons suggested that we came from resilient stock — comforting lore in our

Wayne Hussey and his prizewinning draft mules plow fields in Randolph County the old-fashioned way.

modern lives. This cemetery is, too. It's like a forest mirage, a vision of North Carolina's agrarian past appearing at the very heart of its high-tech present.

But to understand this place, to understand who created it and why, one has to get to know mules.

There was once a time when you'd never have to explain why mules were loved like family in North Carolina, much less *what* they were. But in the span of three generations, that knowledge has disappeared as surely as the furrows they plowed. So, a primer: Mules are the offspring of a horse and a donkey, most often a female horse and a male donkey. They're considered the world's oldest hybrid, first appearing 4,000 years ago in Turkey. They've got all the appropriate parts but an odd number of chromosomes, which means that except in very rare instances, they can't reproduce.

What might be an embarrassing snag for some species is for mules a point of pride. It's their robust combination of inherited traits that makes them so spectacular — the survival instinct of a donkey and the superior ancestry of a horse. Hybrid vigor at its best. Intelligent, sure-footed, hardy,

PHOTOGRAPH BY LISSA GOTWALS

Fabius Page's mules are buried in an unmarked cemetery in what was once Nelson, a small town near Research Triangle Park.

could make. It might treat you like a fool until you earned its trust, but after that, it would work twice as hard as a horse on half the feed. And it would live longer, too. It would carry you to town on Saturday, take your family to church on Sunday, and didn't care for fancy oats; briars would do. The perfect partner when times were tough. As one mule owner I know likes to say, "Mules don't like prosperity."

Most everyone loved their mule, even when it was aggravating.

and discerning. Even Charles Darwin considered the mule a work of art. He wrote in his journal, "That the offspring of the horse and the ass should possess more reason, memory, obstinacy, social affection, powers of muscular endurance, and length of life, than either of its parents, seems to indicate that art has here outdone nature."

Lofty language, sure, for an animal more commonly remembered as hardheaded and bossy. As William Faulkner wrote of the mule, "He will labor ten years patiently for the privilege to kick you once." And yet, there was a time when farmers wouldn't have had it any other way. By the 1920s, half of all North Carolinians lived on farms, and poverty was so pervasive that many didn't even notice when the Great Depression began. A mule was perhaps the best investment one

A mule is only as good as its owner, they say. And most everyone loved their mule, even when it was aggravating. My grandfather included: His last words to my dad, just before he died at age 93, were, "Son, ain't we got a barn full of the *finest* mules?"

WAYNE HUSSEY'S MULES ARE AMONG THE finest in the state. He has ribbons to prove it, though he's not the type to brag. His 15 acres are tilled by mule and plow, which requires equal parts strength and artistry. "I got four or five tractors, but I like mules," says 64-year-old Hussey. Leaning on the barnyard fence, he murmurs, "They're quieter and easier-goin'."

He has females, a sisterhood like at the

cemetery: Josey, Bonnie, Mabel, Jane, and Pat, a 26-year-old mule who belonged to his daddy. Sixteen hands, 1,400 pounds, all five sorrel-colored, with blonde manes trimmed short. These are draft mules: part donkey, part Belgian horse.

Hussey's Randolph County farm is a postcard from mule country, where daylilies line ditches and worn-out tobacco barns lean into the wind. Folks slow down when Hussey and his mules are out working their fields. Unlike tractor rows, mule-plowed rows are lumpy, slightly irregular, and utterly beautiful. Across the loamy soil, he calls out directions to his team: "Gee!" and "Haw!" Once, every farm kid in the state knew those words for right and left. It's strangely reassuring that someone still does.

Between World Wars I and II, as cities grew and big farms swallowed up little farms, mechanization took hold and tractors supplanted mules. North Carolina hung on to mule labor longer than almost any other state, but by 1950 mules were a rare sight in our pastures. Now, their images linger in photographs on the walls of barbecue joints, and in the memories of old-timers like my grandfather.

Hussey's mules live in both worlds: They're working animals, no doubt, but they also travel the country as show mules, which is where the present-day mule is in her glory. Pat even marched in the Tournament of Roses Parade.

FROM THE WOODED CEMETERY WHERE KATE, Lulu, Rose, and Maud are buried, you can hear the din of rush hour traffic to RTP. It wasn't always this busy. This was once farmland. Mules, barns, fields, a small community called Nelson. A tobacco farmer named Fabius Haywood Page, his wife, and their five kids lived here in a two-story, tin-roofed farmhouse, porches front and back. A tall, friendly man, Page spent nearly every day of his 89 years on the family farm — from 1889 to 1978 — on land that's now woods and tombstones.

His mother was a music teacher who filled the house with books. But he had to learn to dodge his father's mean temper. A friendship with the family's mules and horses provided solace. When he was 9 years old, he discovered *Black Beauty*, a heartache of a book narrated by a horse whose bittersweet life experiences moved Page in ways no one would ever quite understand. After reading it, he decided he would never sell a single mule or horse. "I keep them all their life and give them a good burial when they die," he once told a curious reporter.

And he was true to his word. "He never did buy a tractor," says Doris Page Smith, who, at 85 years old, is his last surviving child. "I remember those mules. Rose and Kate especially," she chuckles. "During the winter they would be mostly in the barn. But in the summer he was out all day long in the field with them."

Cedar Fork Baptist Church is about all that's left of Nelson. Almost all of the fields are gone. But Page's animals are there, tucked in the woods, just out of sight: mules on one side, horses on the other. His was a striking act of kindness for which he expected nothing in return. "I have stipulated in my will," he told the same reporter in 1956, "that that piece of property on which the graveyard is located can never be sold or traded. So it'll be there long after I'm gone."

The fact that no one would likely visit these graves after he was gone makes this final expression of gratitude even more touching. For mules, who have no descendants and whose legacy is tied to a generation of farmers now mostly gone, the cemetery is a monument, a memorial to a time when they mattered. — *Robyn Yiğit Smith*

APPEARED IN
2013

Dogs
OF WAR

After they complete their military service, K9 veterans find respect, admiration, and plenty of snuggle time from adoptive families.

PHOTOGRAPH BY ANDREW CRAFT

62

A dog named Doc is doing laps around the coffee table, the two tags on his camouflage collar jingling like quarters in a fidgety man's pocket. His pink tongue hangs out of his mouth as if it could unravel all the way to the floor. Across the street in his neighborhood on the edge of Fayetteville, some kids are laughing and carrying on. Their squeals have Doc, a 78-pound Belgian Malinois, going in circles. Jingle, jingle, jingle. Huff, huff, huff.

But now he stops. He's between my end of the leather sofa and the flat-screen TV. Doc sits with impeccable posture, his eyes glaring out the storm door, his ears extended like two dorsal fins. Except for his rapid-fire breathing, he's as still as a soldier at attention. I look into his brown eyes. The things those eyes have seen. Iraq: been there. Afghanistan: been there. War: done that.

The voices of neighborhood kids have trailed off. Doc is now at ease, though his ears are still erect. Inside one ear, imprinted on that unflappable flap, is a tattoo with an identification number: L258. The things those ears have heard. His wet nose nudges my wrist and advances toward my lap. I know what that face says: What's a dog gotta do for a little back rub around here?

"You sure are one handsome dog," I tell him, stroking his deep-pile coat of black and brown and gray. I can't call him cute or sweet, nor can I engage in baby talk. This is a veteran. An American hero. I should shake his paw, pat his back, say "thank you for your service," and "may God bless you," and "have one on me."

 On his collar, his name is spelled "Ddoc." Lackland Air Force Base, where he was born and trained, doubles the first two letters of a canine's name so dogs from its breeding program can be easily identified.

Doc — or Ddoc, if you will — is a lovable dog in a home where his caretakers give him "snuggle sessions." He has a spacious grass-and-sand backyard, kibble in his bowl, and tennis balls to sink his teeth into. The demands of the battlefield have surrendered to the quaint commands displayed in three words on the fireplace mantel: Live. Laugh. Bark.

IT'S OCTOBER 2011, ON A ROAD SOMEWHERE in Afghanistan. Doc is on patrol with soldiers from Fort Bragg. Tethered to his handler, he's sniffing for improvised explosive devices, better known by their dread abbreviation: IEDs. It's what he's trained to do, and he does his job exceptionally well. His current owner says during his month and a half in Afghanistan, Doc found 14 IEDs. He even detected a pressure plate for a bomb that the Explosive Ordnance Disposal specialists overlooked. Had he not found it ...

Suffice it to say this dog has saved lives.

But then there was a "situation," as his former handler, Staff Sgt. Mike Alcorn, describes it. Alcorn is talking to me on his cell phone in his car in Alexandria, Virginia, where he now lives. "He was not the same dog after that situation," Alcorn says. "He was still my buddy. He was scared to death. He'd run and cower and hide under my cot. He didn't want to go on missions after that."

Doc's new family recounts the "situation" that traumatized him. Doc and his squadron come under attack. There's gunfire. There's mortar fire. One of the mortars strikes so close it hurls Doc and Alcorn some 300 feet, with the handler landing on top of the dog. "And from then on, Doc was trying to pull him away, like 'get out of here!' " says Sgt. Chloe Wells, the 27-year-old soldier from Fort Bragg who adopted Doc.

Doc lived out his retirement with Sgt. Chloe Wells and his new adoptive family in Fayetteville, far from the war zones where he spent his career.

Alcorn tries to return fire, but Doc is pulling his leash the other way. They both end up in a ditch. Alcorn is still trying to return fire, but Doc is yanking too hard. There's no use. Doc wins.

And then it's over.

And then they're back at base.

And then ... *what's wrong with Doc?*

Maybe he just needs some time off. Let's give him some dummy explosives to practice with. He noses them out as expertly as ever, but he's not alerting anyone. He's supposed to sit — why isn't he sitting? We can't trust him to go out and patrol if he's not alerting to anything.

Doc has to go home. By December, he and Alcorn are back in the states. A veterinarian diagnoses Doc with canine post-traumatic stress disorder (PTSD), and he is retired. Alcorn fills out all the papers to adopt him and is so elated at the thought of taking his beloved battle buddy home.

But Alcorn has a baby on the way — Doc doesn't do well around babies — and he's about to move into a smaller house out of state. With two dogs already, a baby, a new job assignment, and a new city, adopting Doc just won't work out. "It's probably one of the hardest decisions I ever made," Alcorn says. "After all we've been through ..."

ALCORN'S VOICE CRACKS AS HE TELLS HIS story. "Man, I cried for days after that. It was terrible, terrible," he says. "I'm getting all choked up thinking about it now."

He moved on, resigned to the thought that he likely would never see Doc again.

Doc was born in March 2006 at Lackland Air Force Base in San Antonio, Texas, home of the Department of Defense Military Working Dog Program. This is where most dogs — mainly Belgian Malinois, German shepherds, and Labrador retrievers — are raised for combat and law enforcement duty in the military. Lackland has about 1,000 dogs at any given time, with anywhere from 500 to 600 on deployment. Of those, roughly 5 percent show signs of canine PTSD, according to Dr. Walter Burghardt, chief of behavioral medicine at Lackland.

Chloe adopted Doc after she came across his picture in March on Craigslist. The ad mentioned that a family could no longer care for Doc, and he needed a new home. With a big heart for big dogs (she already had two, a Belgian Malinois and German shepherd), Chloe had to see Doc for herself. She drove to the animal shelter on Fort Bragg and looked into those brown eyes that have seen so much. "He came right up to me, hopped up, gave me a lick on the face, and put his paw on my shoulder."

Her husband, Sgt. First Class Jeff Wells,

wasn't all warm and fuzzy to the idea of a third dog around the house. But then he saw those eyes, and he heard those stories of Doc's service downrange, and he felt that tug. "I looked at him sitting all handsome and proud. I couldn't help but think he's a war hero who's living in the house," he says.

> "I couldn't help but think he's a war hero who's living in the house."

You watch him there on the hardwood floor, astride the boot-clad feet of his caretakers, doing the things that dogs do — licking, chewing, scratching, panting — and think about what this dog has done. He has his flashbacks and bouts of anxiety, yes, but right now he looks innocent and at peace. As Jeff points out, "It's hard to imagine him being downrange, sniffing out bombs and saving lives."

LIKE MANY OF THEIR MEN AND WOMEN counterparts who go off to war, many four-legged warriors don't come home alive. They, too, had people who cared about them and loved them and cried at their passing. They, too, had names. Bart. Bronco. Freddy. Pepper. On a sunny Saturday in July, Doc was among the bewhiskered faces in the crowd for the unveiling of the Special Operations Forces Canine Memorial. There, outside the Airborne and Special Operations Museum in Fayetteville, a bronze statue of a Belgian Malinois, decked out in combat gear, stands sentinel over 58 granite stones bearing the names of dogs killed in action. Beneath each name — Valco and Falco and Marco and Mailo — is the year and mission in which the dog gave his life. Chiseled in the centerpiece stone are these words: "Here we honor our SOF K9's that have paid the ultimate price."

IT'S MEMORIAL DAY WEEKEND 2013. STAFF Sgt. Mike Alcorn is with his wife, Megan, at the Iwo Jima Memorial outside Washington, D.C. His 7-month-old daughter, Adelynn, is in the stroller. They're out for a walk, ambling among all the other people looking around. And then there's this dog with ears like dorsal fins and a deep-pile coat of black and brown and gray.

Is that ... ?

Like a mother instinctively knows her baby's cry, a handler knows his dog. "My heart just leapt out of my chest," Alcorn says. "Words can't even describe what it meant to me." There he is, with Chloe and Jeff, in this sacred American place, a beautifully fitting place to honor the sacred bond between a soldier and his canine comrade.

But will he recognize me?

Doc is running now. He jumps into his old partner's arms. It feels so good. Alcorn is crying. His wife had been in on the scheme. Chloe and Jeff wanted to drive from Fayetteville and give Alcorn a surprise visit from Doc. "It was pretty emotional for everybody," Chloe tells me.

They visit for an hour or so in the park. Doc and Alcorn have some one-on-one time. Then it's time to go, time for goodbye. Man, is that hard. Alcorn is crying again. Everyone is crying. He loves this dog so much. But it comforts him to know that his old buddy is getting snuggle sessions in a good home where he can live and laugh and bark. Those aren't the only feel-good words above the Wellses' fireplace mantel. Here are two more: Happy Tails. — *Bryan Mims*

APPEARED IN 2018

ONE MAN'S *Palmetto Bug...*

The beach bugs most of us know and loathe aren't nearly as disgusting as they are by their other name.

My daughter, Markie, was a smidge offended, I do believe.

She and a friend were living at our house in Morehead City over the summer, working after their sophomore year in college. Markie said her pal was really freaked out. She'd told Markie: "Your parents need to do something about all these roaches."

I did a double-take. It's not like we're neat freaks, but even I won't tolerate vermin.

"Roaches?" I asked. "We don't have no roaches. We're high-class people. Everybody knows that."

I fact-checked this position with my son.

"Jack," I asked him. "You seen any roaches down at the beach house?"

He never looked up from his iPhone. "Roaches?" he replied. "No. That's nasty."

Julie, my wife, was laughing already. "She must've been talking about the Palmetto bugs," she said. "Those aren't roaches. They're just beach bugs."

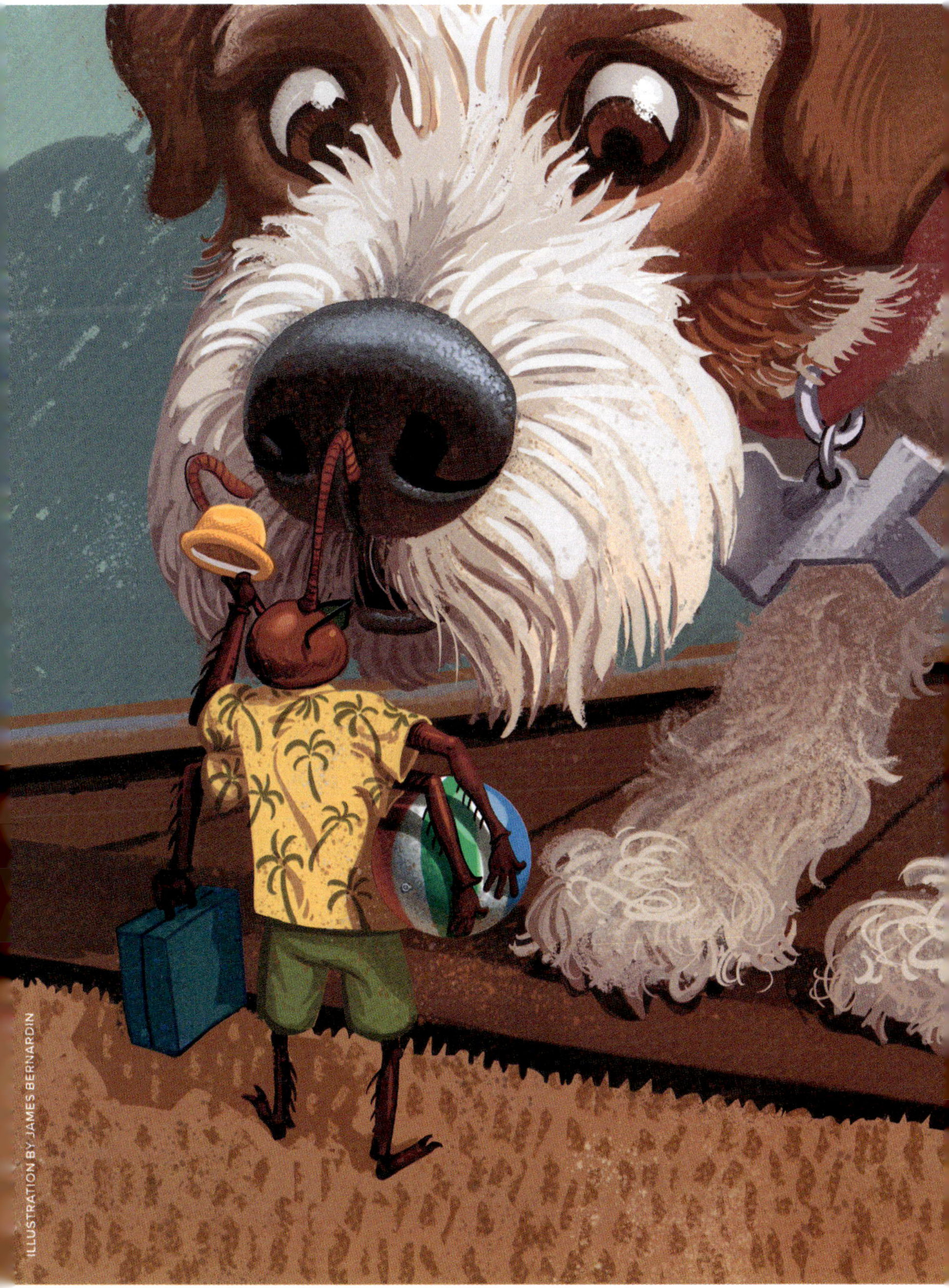

ILLUSTRATION BY JAMES BERNARDIN

"Absolutely not," I said, settling the question. After all, I subscribe to Smithsonian magazine. I'm practically a scientist.

The family breathed a little easier. Just a little misunderstanding. We sure didn't want people thinking we have roaches.

If you have a beach place, or frequent the Cackalacky coast, you know what I'm talking about. Here in polite beach country, the large, multi-segmented insects with the lustrous chocolate-brown exoskeletons are known as Palmetto bugs. Beach bugs. They're as common as sand spurs. Part of the package. They're not roaches — have you lost your mind? Every beach cottage comes with Palmetto bugs. You don't even have to place a special order. Heck, we're on a first-name basis with some of them. Look, there's Fred. I think he's lost another leg, poor boy.

I'll admit that Palmetto bugs can get under your skin. Sort of. We've had to install child-proof locks on a couple of cabinets. One or two Palmetto bugs at our place have learned to open the refrigerator. When they get that big and obstinate, Black Flag won't do. I've resorted to .30-06 rounds. You just gotta watch where you shoot.

But mostly, folks at the coast learn to accommodate. We're not averse to swinging a rolled-up newspaper when we need to, but, like sunburn and sand in the bed, Palmetto bugs — not roaches, fer crying out loud, that's nasty — are just a part of having a beach place.

I think about that exchange with Markie's friend every March or so, when Julie and I head down to Morehead City to open up our beach place. Well, we don't really "open it up" since it's never really closed, and it's not really a beach place since it's three blocks from Bogue Sound in downtown Morehead City. But we do like to roll down in March and get all 950 square feet of it spruced up for the coming spring and summer. For a lot of folks who have a place at the beach or in the mountains or by the lake, it's a pretty common migration this time of year.

Julie immediately goes into some sort of scary deep-clean voodoo trance while I do the important stuff. I take stock of the spice rack — Old Bay, blackening spices for fish and shrimp, barbecue sauce in all the important styles: eastern, Lexington, Memphis, that stuff with Cheerwine in it. I change out the lines in the fishing reels. Oil the bicycle chains. We have our annual argument over the lack of a showerhead in the outdoor shower. A few years back, the showerhead fell off, and now the water roars from the open pipe in a torrent that will knock you into the back wall if you're not ready for it. It's like having a private room at Massage Envy. Jack and I have vowed never to replace it.

> **Palmetto bugs are just a part of having a beach place.**

It takes us most of a Saturday to spit-shine the place and decide that, yes, we do think we can wait another year before painting the porch railings, because in another year, every molecule of paint will have flaked off the railings, and that will make the scraping a whole lot easier. Then we head out to the back porch from which our pooches, Biscuit and Minnie, have watched with complete indifference as their masters work themselves silly. With the kids off to school, it's just the four of us now. Julie brings out her beloved leopard-print electric blanket — I told you we are classy people — and we assume the position: She stretches out on the sofa, feet in my lap, dogs on their blankets, house in order, spring on the way, and we think about the summers past, and that time Markie and I filled the boat with the driftwood that leans against the shed, and the summer Jack had his first crab pots and spent most of an afternoon picking seven crabs on the picnic table. And we wonder about summers to come and pray that we'll all have a chance to be here together, and we drink coffee, and sit quietly in the cold of a March afternoon, still really sort of amazed that we have this place, and that life worked out this way.

Eventually I did spring for the $22-a-month pest-control service. My mom and her friends came to stay at the house one time, and they were, um, less accommodating than I to the gentle pleasantries of the Palmetto bug. "Really," she said, "you have got to do something about those roaches."

But I have to say, I've missed ol' Fred. He hasn't been around to greet me when I raid the fridge for a late-night snack, his glossy back glinting in the light, backed into a corner under the cabinet, antennae twitching as if to say, Hey, man, what's up? Try the crumb cake over by the coffee maker. That stuff is awesome. He never meant any harm. He always scurried into the crevices of the porch sofa when he saw me coming. He was so gracious that way. Always letting me have the good spot. — *T. Edward Nickens*

APPEARED IN 2017

GROWING UP
Carolina

In the Old North State, small moments add up in young minds, and lead to feelings that last a lifetime.

The author's pictures, patches, and books only hint at her memories of growing up in North Carolina.

PHOTOGRAPH BY JOEY SEAWELL

71

After you'd cashed in the bottles littering a construction site and you'd checked for a Buffalo nickel; after stripping the red plastic circle from the bologna slice, and eating the cherry Popsicle your mother halved against the kitchen counter seam; after the squabble when someone cheated at Mother, May I, there was always the dog. You pulled off a tick the size and pearl-gray color of pea gravel, poked it with a stick, then watched the bug wrinkle and deflate. Then it was still just early afternoon in a North Carolina childhood, which also included learning to plait with water-lily stems, feeding lettuce to adopted box turtles, batting hickory nuts with the broken-off end of a croquet mallet, and trying to see if a magnifying glass could really start a fire. Except that you didn't have the patience to find out.

A North Carolina childhood included agonizing decisions: at Tweetsie Railroad, between the braided rawhide whip and the miniature wishing-well bank made of wood, so lacquered that you could see your own reflection. Or, Down East, between the hermit crab and the Venus flytrap, which seemed, frankly, to have more personality, despite being a plant. It was stubbed toes and skinned knees and poison ivy, the only treatment for which was calamine, which you surreptitiously peeled off in flakes when it dried, the better to get back to the satisfactory, single-minded business of rash-scratching.

In hindsight — because, alas, who's aware of childhood while they're living it? — much of a North Carolina childhood is based on school and seasons. During the school year, you went to Raleigh on a class field trip, where the Kleenex sprouting from the wall in a motel room was more wondrous than the State Capitol building. You learned the correct answer to grammar exercises like "(Our/Are) house is made of bricks" and, in assemblies, hollered more than sang, *Hoo-rah! Hoo-rah! The Old North State foreverrrrrr!*

On vacations, you opened your eyes for the first — and last — time in the salty Atlantic. You visited the Biggest Sand Dune in the World at Jockey's Ridge, and the Sanitary Fish Market and Restaurant in Morehead City, feeling suspicious about the name until you sank your teeth into a hush puppy and knew you'd experienced a tangible, tasteable miracle of crunchy/soft, salty/sweet. You went to Vacation Bible School and made fans with tongue depressors and were allowed the unholy privilege of running a lighter along the edges of your "papyrus" scroll to blacken them. You threw your (empty) baby bottle off Blowing Rock because your grandfather promised $25 if you'd give it up before first grade. At Oconaluftee Indian Village, you crouched on a dirt floor inside a teepee, squatting like my father said they had in Okinawa, ears beside knees. I remember Fontana Dam only because I was wearing the slip-on sneakers I'd craved for so long.

A LOT OF CHILDHOOD IS WANTING SOMEthing. Wanting a name like Louisa or Angela, something with a pretty vowel on the end rather than a useless, unfeminine consonant. Wanting to twirl corn on the cob across the stick of butter rather than using a knife. Wanting whipped cream that came out of a can, and to be on a Christmas parade float.

A North Carolina childhood is warnings, too: that swallowed watermelon seeds will grow in your stomach, and that swallowed gum will clog it up. So you went to sleep with Juicy Fruit still in your mouth and, in the morning, used an ice cube to freeze it out of your hair.

Childhood is picking: blackberries and Queen Anne's lace on the side of the road, tomatoes and squash from the garden, guitar strings and elbow scabs. It's kicking: a ball in the side yard, and your sister under the table. If you're a North Carolina kid, you sell: lemonade and found golf balls and handwritten neighborhood newspapers. You build: dams and tree houses and skateboard ramps. You collect, too: birds' nests and arrowheads, sharks' teeth and mica shards. You earn: allowances and good grades and scout badges and 4-H awards, but never the DAR prize. And you learn: sailing knots and saddling a horse, how a bill becomes a law in Raleigh, and how to make a dog play the banjo with his hind leg. If you're lucky, you learn the two-finger whistle in childhood, but if not, you learn to coax a reasonable shriek out of a blade of grass between your thumbs. You learn, as well, about grieving. For dying pets. Grandparents. Summer's end.

FOR ME, CHILDHOOD'S END ARRIVED ONE day in the mail: a reading list for ninth grade. That summer, I traded Frances Hodgson Burnett's English orphans for Charles Dickens's vastly different versions, swapped Narnia for *The Good Earth*'s China, and abandoned the little house on the prairie for *Nicholas and Alexandra*'s Russia. And yet.

Whether you grew up at the beach, in the mountains, or someplace in between, you never forget your first set of wheels.

"Anybody who has survived his childhood has enough information about life to last him the rest of his days," Flannery O'Connor wrote. So it is, surely, for every grown-up North Carolina child, when they remember their first awkward attempts at snowplowing on Beech Mountain, climbing cherry trees in spring to knock down webby caterpillar nests to play with the dozens of squirming creatures, or coming upon a kitchen sink full of floating cucumbers on their way to becoming pickles. If you can't remember, just put your nose to a whirring box fan, and talk. In that echoing, reverberating hum that once so delighted you, you'll hear — faint but definite — those brief years you believed forgotten.

— *Susan Stafford Kelly*

Rock 'N' Roll Quarry

Before the turquoise water rose, submerging the towering walls of an old granite quarry near Ramseur, the secret swimming hole served as a lesson and a warning to a generation of kids growing up in the 1970s.

Mama always told the two Jeffs and me, "Don't go to that rock quarry." But we went anyway. We were 16 years old, licensed to drive, and deaf to any adult warnings that would prevent us from having fun. Warm days had arrived, and as the sun burned brighter outside classroom windows, the long afternoons at Asheboro High School seemed exponentially longer. We were bored, and we were restless. Mama said, "Well, if you go, then don't dive off of those rocks." But we did anyway.

It was the summer of 1976, and the old granite rock quarry in the rolling countryside between Ramseur and Coleridge was the place to be if you wanted to play hooky on Fridays. We packed my green Toyota Corolla with a cooler and towels, cranked the windows down, shoved a Led Zeppelin eight-track tape into the console, and cruised out of town on U.S. Highway 64, wailing, "You need coolin', baby, I'm not foolin'." In Ramseur, we hung a right onto Coleridge Road, drove past the old mill houses and the little country store where we stopped to buy ice for the cooler; over velvety green pillows of pastureland that extended to the horizons; and on toward the tiny community of Parks Crossroads, where we barely came to a standstill at the four-way stop sign. There,

ILLUSTRATION BY JIM SALVATI

we began looking out for the little dirt road that led to the Promised Land: granite cliffs that towered some 60 feet above a turquoise blue swimming hole stretching more than two football fields long.

We weren't the only ones there when I pulled the car around and parked where the narrow dirt road opened to a small beach at the water's edge. Tim Yates, with his big mane of long, curly brown hair, was leaning against the fender of his 1968 VW Squareback mounted with a powerful sound system that blared blues-rock music across the crystalline surface. Others were stretched out on huge tractor-tire inner tubes, floating amid the massive rock walls and sipping from cans wrapped in Styrofoam can coolers. I won't say what any of us were drinking because, at 16, it might have been illegal. But I will say that, in the late '70s, Friday at the rock quarry was the best party in Randolph County.

Wearing T-shirts, flip-flops, and cut-off jeans, the two Jeffs and I hopped out of the car and ambled around the edge of the quarry, past a rope swing on one side and on to the opposite end, where one of the tallest cliffs formed a natural platform for diving. I was fearless in those days. Standing at a little point that jutted out from the other rocks, I raised both arms high in the air and let out a hearty yell that ricocheted off the granite walls. Then I lunged forward. I could barely make out the wavering guitars from Tim's sound system as I hurled myself down and splashed into the coldest water I'd ever felt. It took my breath away. We climbed back up and jumped from that cliff over and over until we were exhausted. Eventually, we retreated to inner tubes to relax and stare up at the jagged walls that formed the most beautiful frame you could imagine for the blue Carolina sky and its little puffy clouds. The lyrics of a Fleetwood Mac song warbled across the shimmering surface: "I turned around and the water was closing all around like a glove ... through the crystal-like and clear water fountain." I remember thinking, *This must be what total freedom feels like.*

THE OLD QUARRY HAD BEEN DUG AT SOME point in the 1960s or early '70s, according to Randolph County Manager Hal Johnson. The North Carolina Department of Transportation mined the gravel for highway construction. Tax records show that the 26 acres of land that the quarry sat on belonged to the Ernest Edward Burgess family in 1972, and it seems to have been in that family since the '20s. It was later owned by John Duvall. But we never thought much about the quarry's origins, or who owned it, when we swam there during our high school years. We knew that it was illegal to be there, but none of the other stuff mattered. What *did* matter to us were the legends: We'd heard that bodies had been found in the quarry, and that stolen cars and other hot items were lodged in the rocks at the bottom. I didn't believe much of it at the time, but as it turns out, some stories were true.

I remember thinking, *This must be what total freedom feels like.*

"We retrieved several stolen vehicles over the years," Larry Pugh wrote in a Facebook group about those summers at the quarry. Pugh served as chief of the Ash-Rand Rescue Squad during the 1980s. "There's a '65 Chevrolet still in the quarry, and a crushed VW." He said he once found a bicycle submerged under a rock. "I often wondered if someone had been riding it," he wrote. In one summer alone, Pugh retrieved 97 pairs of sunglasses, a "small fortune" in aluminum cans stuffed under a floating wooden platform in the middle of the pond, and an unopened gallon of Jack Daniel's whiskey.

The quarry may have been a glorious secret spot for teenagers from the surrounding small towns — Asheboro, Siler City, Coleridge — to swim and to get away from the grind of long, hot school days, but it was not without controversy. Some kids would take risks that landed them in the hospital or worse. Members of motorcycle clubs would show up and swagger about as if they owned the place. Neighbors complained of the loud music and mischief. One person on Facebook remembered an Asheboro High School assistant principal following students to the quarry to bring them back to school. All of this explains why Mama had warned the Jeffs and me not to go to the quarry. But for many of us, going to the quarry was an integral part of teen life in the '70s. It played an important role in our coming of age. We were learning to make choices — some of them good, others not so good.

TODAY, WHEN I LOOK BACK ON THAT SUMMER when the two Jeffs and I frequented the quarry, I like to think of one of the last good days. It wasn't much different from any other day: I was floating on an inner tube, Tim Yates was leaning against the fender of that VW, and the sky was bluer than heaven. And like every afternoon at the quarry back then, the day ended the same way, the same song blasting from the sound system: guitar gods Eric Clapton and Duane Allman churning away on the rock anthem "Layla." Over time, that song had become a tradition at the quarry. "The tapes that I played the most were The Allman Brothers' live *At Fillmore East*, Peter Frampton, *Led Zeppelin IV*, and B.B. King," Tim recently recalled. "But the last song that I would always play was 'Layla' — that got to be my leaving trademark."

And one of my dear late mother's enduring trademarks? "Don't go to that rock quarry." But we did anyway. — *Mark Kemp*

APPEARED IN
2016

THE SCHOOL OF Basketball

If you didn't go to the ACC Tournament, the games came to you, even in the classroom.

This story takes place in a time before Duke fans had been invented. It's true. In the 1980s, at Farmington Woods Elementary School in Cary, we did not know any Duke fans. We knew Carolina fans and we knew NC State fans. That was it. Although I had seen them on television and therefore assumed they existed — probably somewhere far away, like New Jersey — I did not personally know an actual Duke fan until ninth grade.

It was Carolina or State. You had to choose. You couldn't root for both.

There were two rites of passage among Farmington Woods students. There was "swish," a bizarre, mint-green fluoride mouthwash that was universally despised. Approximately once every two weeks, teachers would pass out tiny plastic cups, and students would spend 30 seconds of class time swishing and spitting into them. Look, no one said the 1980s made sense.

ILLUSTRATION BY JAMES BENNETT

79

The other was basketball. Most of us were natives (I told you this was a long time ago) so we already had built-in allegiances. We had, therefore, a solid supply of sweatshirts declaring our favorite team, which enabled us to participate in elementary school Atlantic Coast Conference (ACC) combat. This meant, of course, that if your team won, you wore the victorious team's sweatshirt on the day after it beat the other team, and then you acted as obnoxiously as possible.

As a young Tar Heel fan — one who was vocal about my loyalty — there was nothing in the world worse than knowing I would have to go to school the next day and face a sea of Wolfpack sweatshirts. In 1987, after NC State defeated Carolina in the ACC championship game, purely to avoid the teasing I knew would ensue, I convinced three State fans at school the following day that the game's outcome had been vacated due to some nebulous rules violation. It was one of my finest elementary school achievements. Sometimes life without the Internet was pretty great.

"I know Coach Smith is a great coach," my dad would say occasionally, "but I'm not sure he understands how tough it is to live so close to Raleigh and deal with all the State fans." If only we could explain it to Dean Smith, he would do something different in the final 30 seconds of the game, just so my father and I would not have to deal with those pesky NC State fans. I could just hear Coach Smith in the huddle with the team: "I'm really worried about Jim and Adam having to go to work and school tomorrow. Let's go ahead and give the ball to J.R. Reid."

On the first Friday of every March, something amazing happened: the ACC Tournament. This was not the bloated 14-team tournament we know today. There were only eight teams. We knew every player and every coach. We knew the scores of every conference matchup during the regular season. We knew that Tom E. Smith would do the Food Lion commercials during the game and that Dinah Shore would award the Holly Farms Player of the Game afterward.

The teachers — let me rephrase that, the cool teachers — knew that we knew. And so, when ACC Tournament games began on Friday at noon on WRAL-TV ("The Big Five," as WRAL sportscaster Tom Suiter called it), the cool teachers would arrange for a television to be wheeled into the classroom.

The teachers — the cool teachers — would arrange for a television to be wheeled into the classroom.

Yes, kids, TVs had to be wheeled. Televisions weren't standard equipment in our classrooms. They had to be signed out from the media center, and then two lucky kids would be excused from class to fetch the tall black cart that had a behemoth TV set on top. They would wheel the cart down the hall and position it at the front of the classroom. And there would be basketball.

In the fourth grade, I had a cool teacher. Her name was Cecelia Chapman, and she was the teacher everyone at Farmington Woods wanted for fourth grade. Rumor had it that my mother had made a pointed "request" for me to land in Mrs. Chapman's class after a rough third grade year. Whatever it takes.

Mrs. Chapman, of course, was the kind of teacher who would reserve a television at the media center well in advance of ACC Tournament Friday. Thirty years later, I caught up with her on the phone. Despite my classroom behavior in the mid-1980s, she stayed in education and went on to have a decorated career, including seven years as the principal of Leesville Road Elementary School in Raleigh.

"Math is not always the favorite subject of a lot of kids," she says. "So as a teacher, who wouldn't jump at the opportunity to get kids excited to see how math can be utilized in the real world through watching the ACC Tournament?"

Mrs. Chapman passed out permission slips before the Friday of the ACC Tournament, informing parents there would be basketball on TV in a future class. And yes, some parents wouldn't sign the form. These people, in the mid-1980s, were better known as Communists. Their failure to give permission exiled their kids to a separate classroom with an unfortunate teacher who, presumably, drew the short straw, and those poor students would do non-basketball-themed lessons.

That didn't render those exiles completely immune from living on Tobacco Road. One year, after Carolina won the ACC championship, the Farmington Woods music teacher organized an impromptu band of Tar Heel fans to parade through the halls of the school, playing the UNC fight song on the only instrument available: recorders. Carolina fans lined the halls to clap along. This was how a generation of college basketball fans were nurtured.

Two of my children, a son and a daughter, were taught by Claire Nelson at Rashkis Elementary in Chapel Hill during the past five years. Mrs. Nelson is also a cool teacher.

She does not, however, have to sign up to have a television wheeled into the classroom on the day of the ACC Tournament quarterfinals. She's been known to use tournament games to teach multiplication. There's a rumor that another teacher in the school might even organize an NCAA Tournament pool (purely for entertainment purposes).

Admittedly, it's not completely instructional time. But ACC Tournament time is guaranteed to include some of the most-remembered days of the school year.

"Instead of academic lessons, I think the kids are learning more about life lessons," Nelson says. "I can wear a UNC shirt, you can wear a Duke shirt, and we can still cheer for our teams and be respectful."

That's right — they have Duke fans in schools now. I hope they all have to swish.

— *Adam Lucas*

APPEARED IN
2016

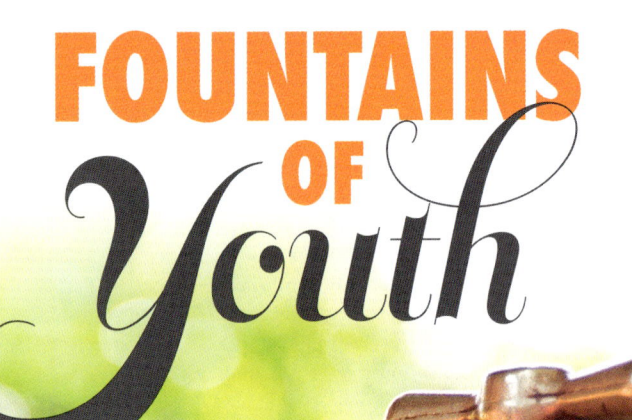

FOUNTAINS
OF
Youth

In North Carolina, that outside faucet is called a "spicket," not a spigot, and it provides more than just water. It's the source of childhood memories of summer.

Every North Carolina kid knows that a spicket is just a hose and a sprinkler away from hours of refreshing entertainment.

No, it's not a spigot. Don't care what your spell check says: It's a spicket. That ungraceful, unlovely outside faucet — often inconveniently located behind shrubbery — is nevertheless essential to life. Because the spicket is the source of life-giving water, in gushes and drips.

Conquering the spicket handle is one of the first triumphs of childhood, right up there with learning left from right: Once you grasp *lefty loosey, righty tighty*, not only can you get yourself a drink without going inside, but you'll also take this skill into the wider world, mastering ketchup bottles and pickle jars. All thanks to the humble spicket, whose ridged, gridded, unyielding handle left dents and red imprints on your palm as you wrestled with its intractability.

Intractable, because your brother had twisted the handle tightly to thwart your thirst, and to make sure you couldn't fill up water balloons. A spicket is *made* for water balloons. The metal mouth is just the right size, and the screw rings grip a balloon's stem almost as well as they hang on to hose nozzles.

Childhood summers in North Carolina pretty much revolved around a spicket, and they still do. You'd screw on the hose and spray each other. You'd call your sister over to help you with the spicket, and as she leaned over to examine the problem, you'd press your thumb to the opening, drenching her with the spray. When she went to tattle, you'd collapse laughing, knowing your mother would never come outside to scold you, because summer outside is lawless.

My grandmother's spicket in Walnut Cove stuck out of the lawn on a metal pipe, about knee high. We'd pull the wading pool right underneath that spicket to fill it, no need for a hose. Then we'd lie on our backs and turn on the water, which cooled our foreheads and scalps.

SPICKETS ARE FOR FILLING WATER GUNS, watering cans, and the dog's bowl. For washing the slivers of grass from your bare feet after you've run through the just-mowed lawn. For rinsing paintbrushes and trowels and shells, and cleaning red clay off the bottom of your sneakers. For washing the car, and filling the Mason jar for field-picked flowers. Hunters and fishermen from Morganton to Morehead City: You'd best clean your game, your fish, and your equipment at the spicket, not at the kitchen tap. Trust me on this.

The little black circles that pop up at the edges of lawns like gophers? Those are not spickets. They are "irrigation systems," and they bear no resemblance to the unpretentious spicket. In Rutherfordton, my parents eventually had a pool put in our backyard. Our well, though, didn't pump enough water per minute to fill it. The solution? A spicket, of course. Inch by inch, to a 10-foot depth beneath the diving board, our pool was filled via a dozen connected hoses attached to a single spicket at our neighbor's house, a half-mile through the woods. The spicket: Lowly in location, but essential in function.

Make a vow to take a drink from a spicket sometime soon. Just remember that it takes time for small hands to master the handle, so if you please, leave it a wee bit *lefty loosey*.

— *Susan Stafford Kelly*

APPEARED IN
2015

UP IN THE
Clouds

Welcome to Boone, the Southern mountain town whose personality is in its precipitation.

In Boone, people sometimes include a disclaimer when making promises: *God willing and the creeks don't rise.* Why, you ask? Tonight is your answer. The creeks have been pulled from their banks as if by strange music. They're falling, dancing and drunken, into the South Fork of the New River, which runs just beyond my back door. Nearby, a paved road has already been covered by its currents. My gravel drive — an earthen dam holding a pond — is in danger. And the rains keep coming down.

PHOTOGRAPH BY TOMMY WHITE

The shops on King Street in downtown Boone maintain a cheerful glow — even under a layer of snow.

It's not uncommon to hear people discussing what makes a place Southern. But when it comes to Boone, I think the question might be: What makes it Southern *Appalachian*? What constitutes its marrow, its personality? My suggestion: precipitation. If humidity is Southern, then earth-moving floods and mountain-size snowfalls are Southern Appalachian. Precipitation, in its many forms, feeds mountain creeks, covers ski slopes, plays midwife to the salamanders that wiggle in my palm when lifted from dark, moist soil.

Boone might be the only town I know that's defined less by what's inside of its municipal borders than by how it reflects what's outside of them. Visitors might go downtown for restaurants and shopping, but the real reasons they've come to Boone are revealed on their roof racks, in the form of kayaks, river tubes, Christmas trees, skis, and snowboards. Trace these tourist icons far enough, and they'll all praise some form of precipitation.

This evening, dusk has turned to darkness quickly. I walk out to check how high the river has gotten. I want to see — best as I can by flashlight beam — whole logs being moved like toothpicks. In a matter of hours, my highland yard has become a swamp. I move to where the waters are lapping at the silvered locust posts of my garden fence. Beyond, there are surf-worthy waves. I can hear and feel them, their power surging with my heart rate.

Later, I lie fitful in bed, listening. What is happening out there? The river sounds like a freight train barreling just inches away from my head. Is this the sound of my road turned to silt? My house is on high ground. There is nothing left to do but wait out the storm. Still, it's hard to rest, my soul pulled toward the river like tides to the moon.

Discontent to stay behind rain-whipped windows, I shuffle onto the back porch with a quilt wrapped around my shoulders. The air smells as it does after the garden's first spring tilling, all fresh earth and possibility. Tonight, across town at the Boone Mall, a car will be lost to an adjacent creek, but stores will be spared. Ultimately, so will my road. But the landscape will be slightly different. Riverbanks shift. Mountainsides slip. Here, beauty does not always arrive gently.

Living in Boone means watching the weather, sometimes on a minute-by-minute basis.

The long-range views from Boone can make one feel small. So can the realization that, in this ancient landscape, not everything is under human control. Just as these mountains tend to make people feel either suffocated or cradled, Boone's oft-extreme precipitation can be viewed as either frightening or empowering. Because it demonstrates that we're undeniably a part of nature, something larger than ourselves.

To feel ice freckling your cheeks is to be part of a geologic story that has transformed the Appalachians — once as high as the Alps and Rockies — into serene scenes. Jagged peaks have been softened, over millions of years, by pelting ice and slow erosion. Rain- and snow-fed rivers continue to deepen valleys. On the ridgelines around town, you can walk right through clouds, in the form of fog, on a near-daily basis. At 3,333 feet above sea level, surrounded by temperate rainforest, Boone is part of an ongoing drama that rivals any story orated by the ancient Greeks.

The App Terrain Park at Appalachian Ski Mountain between Boone and Blowing Rock is always evolving, to keep the course challenging.

TONIGHT'S RAIN IS SWELLING THE HEART-OF- town flow of Kraut Creek, saturating the grassy lawns of Appalachian State University. It's making puddles in parks, deepening cracks in asphalt. Rain is what makes the woods around town feel like fern-draped, prehistoric areas. Leaves that are dripping with moisture are, after all, usually laden with life. And, soon, there'll be new mushrooms growing between brick and sidewalk, in the dark recesses of logs and fallen branches.

Shape-shifting forms of precipitation don't allow locals to get comfortable for too long. They refuse to let us forget that we're tied to a world beyond the one we've created. In the fall, some of us mark foggy days by dropping beans into Mason jars, each bean an indicator of how many snows we might expect in the coming season. Precipitation reminds us to take our raincoats and buy snow tires, tells us how high woodpiles should be stacked and how many canned goods should be stocked. We might get our rations at Food Lion instead of the Mast General Store, but we're still mountaineers.

My neighbors and I mark seasons with cider press parties, potlucks, and picking sessions on the porch of the community center, all timed to coincide with the sort of precipitation we see coming. In turn: Fog rolls through town, thickening with woodstove smoke. Ice glazes trees. Snow coats buildings, presses against roofs. There's the hush after blizzards pass, the crack and moan of slicks breaking, snow slipping off of metal roofs. Then, the sun shines while clouds mist, causing rhododendron to detonate into color, inspiring songbirds to echo *glory, glory* in even the darkest of hollers.

Living in Boone means watching the weather, sometimes on a minute-by-minute basis. We're alert to precipitation because we have to be. Roads close. Slopes open. Bridges are overtaken. Sometimes, we keep watch joyfully. Sometimes, nervously. Almost always, while muttering under our breath about the never-ending onslaught of rain, fog, sleet, and snow. Because it seems that, when it comes to places and people, the things we love most about them are often the very same things that drive us mad. So it goes.

Dawn is still hours away from where I stand. I draw my quilt close to my chest. I can't see very far into my yard, but my senses are attuned. I inhale the strange sweetness of Boone's lifeblood. And the river that usually lulls me to sleep roars me awake. — *Leigh Ann Henion*

Students at Appalachian State University get used to seeing a lot of wintry precipitation on campus: Boone gets an average of 34 inches of snow per year.

APPEARED IN
2013

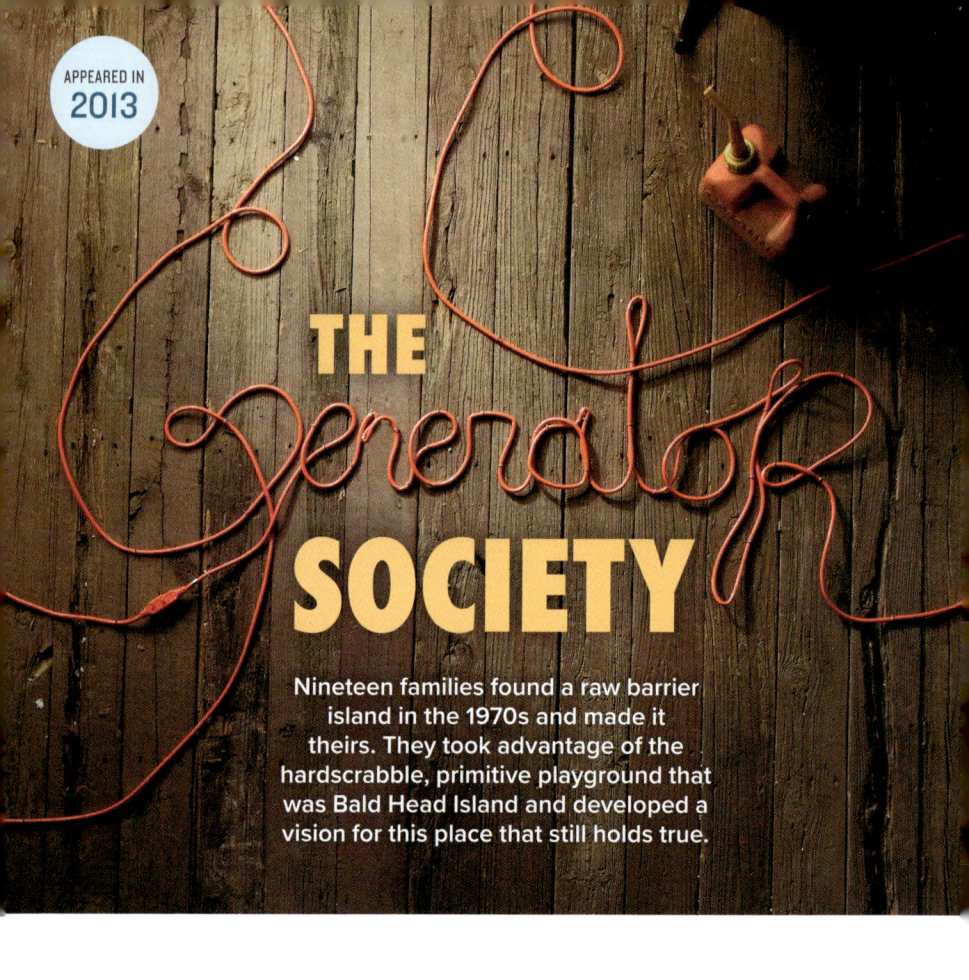

THE *Generator* SOCIETY

Nineteen families found a raw barrier island in the 1970s and made it theirs. They took advantage of the hardscrabble, primitive playground that was Bald Head Island and developed a vision for this place that still holds true.

One of the southernmost parts of the Old North State, one of the northernmost points of this country's subtropics, hard where the warmer, calmer waters of the Cape Fear River clash with the colder, roiling currents of the Atlantic Ocean, Bald Head Island juts into the sea toward the treacherous Frying Pan Shoals. Barrier islands are as much the former as the latter — they are barriers — and so they bear the brunt of the surroundings' relentless assault. The water and the wind spray tiny shards of salt and sand. The dunes get hit first. They protect the maritime forest. The maritime forest gets hit next. It protects the marsh. A healthy barrier island has these three environments, needs all three, disparate but dependent, and the forest in particular is the most important piece of this delicate alchemy of reciprocity.

On Bald Head, the forest is atypically lush, verdant with red cedar and cabbage palmetto, wild olive and American holly, yaupon and loblolly pine, and finally the linchpin laurel and live oaks. The enduring species of trees sport hardy, waxy leaves,

PHOTOGRAPH BY MATT HULSMAN

resistant to the corrosive, airborne swirl — but just as important, maybe even more so, they grow in groups, like flocks of birds or schools of fish, better and more able together than they would be alone, and they form a dense, protective canopy. They interact. They cling to each other, and they move as a unit, their branches reaching to touch.

It's almost as if the trees hold hands because it's how they survive, and they know they won't if they don't.

TO THIS ISLAND CAME 19 FAMILIES IN THE 1970s. They weren't the first people to come to Bald Head. Small, mostly intermittent populations in the past had found their way — Indians looking for food, pirates looking for loot, Civil War conscripts from both sides, lighthouse keepers and Coast Guard rescuers, day fishers and hog hunters, soldiers to test their skills and Boy Scouts to set up camp. Developers came, too, in different decades and eras, all of whom had wide eyes and big plans. Mostly, though, blueprints stayed blueprints, drawn but not built, which is why the 19 families found what they found. They arrived from Lumberton and Raleigh and High Point and Southport and Hendersonville and Hickory and Concord and Cary and Charlotte and Winston-Salem and Virginia and Connecticut. They were doctors and professors and owners of businesses and presidents of companies and publishers of newspapers. They showed up in Penn Yan motorboats driven into the middle of the island on a shallow creek in the couple of hours on either side of high tide because any other time didn't work.

There was no marina. There was no electricity. There were no restaurants or stores. There were no country clubs or swimming pools. There were no phones. The roads were loose sand paths. Empty lots were priced at please please buy, at $15,000, at $11,000, at $10,000.

They loaded precut boards and beams on rented boats, these 19 families, so they could build their Bald Head homes. They sometimes lost appliances and furnishings on river crossings that turned unexpectedly rough. They had tug-pushed barges that ran straight onto beaches with labeled lumber wrapped, so it wouldn't warp in the wetness. They had four-wheel-drive Scout jeeps with half-inflated tires, so they wouldn't get stuck in the sand. They followed simple plans to erect unostentatious homes. There were a couple of houses here and a couple of houses there, until all of them were living hidden behind the dunes or overlooking the marsh or nestled within the thick of the forest.

> **They cling to each other, and they move as a unit, their branches reaching to touch.**

When the families were finished, when they had moved into their second and seasonal homes, they used gas-powered washers and dryers and fridges and stoves. They used gravity-fed water tanks or wells in their yards. They used candles on tables and kerosene lanterns hung on hooks on the walls. The Cunninghams ran a car-battery-powered black-and-white TV, and the Dunlaps did the same with a stereo, settling on a soundtrack of James Taylor and the Eagles, John Prine and Jackson Browne. They used generators, too, all of them did, of all shapes, sizes, and kinds.

When *The State Port Pilot* reported the arrival of power to Bald Head Island on January 28, 1981, residents knew the community they had created was about to change.

They turned them on when they needed power and turned them off when they didn't.

And they had CB radios. They gave their houses names — Skylark and Hilltop and Neptune, Sandfiddler and Sand Dollar and the Raccoon Hilton, Blue Crab and C Turtle and the Seven Cs, Tree House and Pilot House and Happy House — and they tuned their CBs to the same single frequency. All of them did. So everybody could hear everybody.

Anybody need anything?

Anybody have extra gas?

Anybody got any limes?

They were on the island. They were not alone. Eventually, together, they would come to call themselves the Generator Society.

THEY ALL "KNEW," BILL BERNE WROTE, ELEC-tricity was on the way, certain to come "any day." But 1972 became 1973. And 1973 became 1974. And 1974 became 1975. And that's the way it was for the rest of the decade. Even as the developer put in the beginning of a proper marina, even after the greens on the golf course were finally finished, the power on Bald Head Island came from something else.

In the meantime, the families brought most of their food from the mainland in cardboard boxes and coolers: beets, tomatoes, and niblet corn in cans. They brought steaks, too, but were sure to cook them fast because they didn't keep. What they didn't buy they caught, fishing the creeks with nets and the ocean with poles, feasting on bountiful flounder, trout, and drum. They clammed and crabbed and musseled.

They went for jogs and spotted sunning alligators and foxes. They watched loggerhead sea turtles trudge up onto the sand to lay their eggs and then used mesh wire to protect the nests from hungry raccoons. They picked up the prettiest shells.

They gathered frequently for cocktails, cherishing ice cubes, calling them "Bald Head diamonds." They played golf in spikes and nothing else just because they could.

Or so goes the story.

So many stories.

There was the time the Bunns stayed on the island during a hurricane and took cover in Old Baldy, the state's oldest standing lighthouse, but still plenty sturdy, and they climbed the 108 steps to the windowed tip-top, where it was only them and a roosting white owl, and they all watched in awe of such breathtaking power.

There was the time Charlotte Dunlap got a big, rusty fishhook lodged in the meat of

PHOTOGRAPH BY CHRIS HANNANT

her calf, and Thad Wester, a pediatrician back in Lumberton, put her on a picnic table on a porch and turned spot-duty surgeon, albeit one drinking a beer, which was fine because so was the patient, and so was Pat Thomas, who serenaded the scene while playing his accordion.

"Very soon a tremendous camaraderie existed and a closeness that is usually achieved only after many years of friendship," Bippi Grubbs said in the collected recollections.

"We really needed each other back then, took care of each other, appreciated each other," Bynum Tudor said in an oral history interview done a few years ago and recorded by current resident Marilyn Ridgeway.

"Depended on each other," Charlotte Dunlap said, growing in groups, branches reaching to touch.

ELECTRICITY WAS COMING. THIS TIME IT WAS real. It was May of 1980. Carolina Power & Light was saying soon. Thad Wester made jambalaya for a meeting of the property owners on the island. He and some of the others recognized the significance of this shift.

He gave framed certificates to the 19 families that were playful but not frivolous.

"During the early years of Development and Modernization of Bald Head Island," the certificates read, "there were families who endured Inconvenience and Privation in exchange for the Privilege of Being Married to Bald Head in a unique way known only to a few. In Recognition of those families and their Accomplishments, they are hereby declared Members in Perpetuity in …

"THE GENERATOR SOCIETY."

The headline in Southport's *State Port Pilot*, on January 28, 1981: "Lights On At Bald Head As Power Line Complete."

The report quoted Thad Wester.

He talked about "safety, convenience and desirability" — but the advent of the ease of buttons pushed and switches flicked, he added, "causes mixed emotions, for we realize that reliable power will attract many more people …"

The generators weren't the point, only "a common bond," he later wrote in a letter to his grandchildren. "The idea of the Generator Society actually had less to do about generators than it did with the people who chose to pioneer those early years at Bald Head. … Not a single one of them failed to develop an emotional relationship with the island. All realized how fragile the beautiful ecosystems on Bald Head are … and supported all measures to guarantee that we will return the island to our children's children as near like we found it as possible."

BALD HEAD TODAY IS NOT PRECISELY WHAT it was. There's a post office. There's a grocery store. There's a country club with a fitness center that offers yoga and Pilates. There's a reliable ferry that runs every hour and people wait for it by looking at their iPhones. But there's no minigolf. No movie house. No blocks of condos stacked on sand like games of Jenga. And there aren't any cars, only golf carts. Bald Head is a hard place to be in a hurry.

The Generator Society? Most of them are gone. They've moved back to the mainland to be closer to medical care, or they've moved to Florida to be warmer in the winter. Many of them are dead.

It remains an appropriate name, though, the Generator Society, an earned name, even now, maybe especially now, because they started something on Bald Head that has not ended. Is not over.

— *Michael Kruse*

APPEARED IN 2014

CLIMBING
Mount
Mitchell

Eight out of 10 days, this view from the top of Mount Mitchell is obscured by clouds. But anytime you stand here, at the highest point east of the Mississippi River, and gaze outward, your perspective will change.

I sit near the top of North Carolina, not far from the summit of Mount Mitchell, the tallest peak east of the Mississippi River. As I look out, the mountain captivates me. I've never seen a view like this: rain, clouds, sun, and shadow, all at once, like the weather has the attention span of a 4-year-old. It's changing so quickly, I think of the old saying: If you don't like the weather, wait 15 minutes. Here on Mount Mitchell, the weather changes if you walk 15 feet.

What I'm about to do makes little sense: I will drive a few thousand feet down the mountain, and take a long hike back up in the rain, straight through that angry nature.

There's something about ascending to the top of a mountain. Few people wax poetic about descending into deep valleys. Fewer still get misty-eyed about a long walk across the plains. But there are countless odes to the joys of reaching new heights.

As I climb, I think about why.

The observation deck at the tip-top of Mount Mitchell provides a stunning panoramic view of the surrounding mountains.

Overcoming fear is part of it. The higher you climb, the farther you could fall. And the very name of this mountain should make anyone who climbs it stop and think about what they are doing and why.

Mount Mitchell gets its name from Elisha Mitchell, a professor at the University of North Carolina in the early and mid-1800s. In 1835 Mitchell declared that the mountain was the tallest east of the Mississippi River. He calculated the height using barometer readings taken at the top and syncing them with readings taken elsewhere.

Mitchell measured other mountains in the area, and his claims about their heights caused confusion and controversy. He climbed the mountain that now bears his name several more times to retake the measurements. On June 27, 1857, Mitchell, alone at the peak, got lost. When he didn't return, a search party spent several days looking for him. A mountain man named

93

Mount Mitchell is often draped in clouds and fog, but on a clear day, its summit offers views as far as 85 miles.

PHOTOGRAPH BY TOM MOORS

ABOUT THE WRITERS

SHERI CASTLE is a writer, recipe developer, cooking teacher, and the host of *The Key Ingredient*, an Emmy Award-winning show on PBS NC. She is a frequent contributor to *Our State*.

MATT CROSSMAN is a freelance writer. He spent 13 years at the *Sporting News*, and his work has been noted in the *Best American Sports Writing*, *Best American Essays*, and *Year's Best Sports Writing* anthologies nine times.

LEIGH ANN HENION is a *New York Times* bestselling author and writer based in western North Carolina. Her work has won multiple Lowell Thomas Awards from the Society of American Travel Writers.

SCOTT HULER is the senior staff writer at *Duke Magazine* and the author of seven books. He lives in Raleigh.

SUSAN STAFFORD KELLY is a Rutherfordton native, the author of five novels and a collection of essays, and a frequent contributor to *Our State*. She lives in Greensboro.

MARK KEMP is an Asheboro native, an author, a former music editor of *Rolling Stone*, and a senior editor at *Our State*.

MICHAEL KRUSE is an award-winning journalist and senior staff writer for *POLITICO*. He lives in Davidson.

ADAM LUCAS is the author or co-author of nine books about North Carolina basketball, the co-host of the *Carolina Insider* podcast and the senior columnist for GoHeels.com. He lives in Chapel Hill.

JEREMY MARKOVICH is a former *Our State* editor and is currently the communications director for the Program for Leadership and Character at Wake Forest University.

BRYAN MIMS is a freelance writer based in Atlanta and a former reporter for WRAL.

T. EDWARD NICKENS is a contributing editor for *Garden & Gun*, the editor-at-large for *Field & Stream*, and a *New York Times* bestselling author. His column, Ramblin' Man, appears monthly in *Our State*. He lives in Raleigh and Morehead City.

MICHAEL PARKER is the author of eight novels and three collections of stories. He is the recipient of several awards, including the North Carolina Award for Literature. He taught for 27 years in the creative writing program at UNC Greensboro.

DREW PERRY is the author of two books, teaches writing at Elon University, and is a frequent contributor to *Our State*. His column, A Year in This House, appears monthly in the magazine.

JOE POSNANSKI is the *New York Times* bestselling author of six books, an award-winning sportswriter, a two-time Sports Emmy Award winner, and the co-host of *The PosCast* podcast. He lives in Charlotte.

ELEANOR SPICER RICE is a Goldsboro native, an entomologist, and the author of seven books. She lives in Raleigh.

ROBYN YIĞIT SMITH is a freelance writer and documentary film producer. She lives in Chapel Hill.

TOMMY TOMLINSON is an author and freelance writer who lives in Charlotte, where he is also the host of the WFAE podcast *SouthBound*. He spent 23 years as a reporter and local columnist for the *Charlotte Observer*, where he was a finalist for the 2005 Pulitzer Prize in commentary.

LYNN WELLS is a personal chef with more than 20 years of experience in the food and hospitality industry. She is *Our State*'s recipe developer.

TO ORDER MORE

If you've enjoyed *Our State Greatest Hits*, think of your family members, friends, and coworkers who would enjoy it, too! Call the Our State Store at (800) 948-1409, or visit ourstatestore.com.

Big Tom Wilson, who had led Mitchell's initial climb up the mountain, finally discovered his trail and followed it to a creek that led to a waterfall. He looked down and saw Mitchell's body in a pool of water at the bottom. Mitchell had fallen off a ledge, hit his head, and drowned. Historians believe that as darkness fell, he tried to hurry off the mountain.

> **I climbed so close to the clouds that I felt like I stood among them.**

The trail to the summit that exists today climbs 3,600 feet over 5.6 miles, a steady but not treacherous hike, much safer than the one Mitchell followed. At no point does the trail go so near a ledge that hikers could fall off. Still, Mount Mitchell is as rugged a place as you'll find in North Carolina. In a letter to his fiancée that he sent shortly after starting work in Chapel Hill, Elisha Mitchell described the geography of North Carolina: "Here you are presented with a vast ocean of forest."

Early in the 1900s, logging started to drain this vast ocean of forest. That led Gov. Locke Craig and the state legislature to create the state park system, with Mount Mitchell becoming North Carolina's first park, 1,946 acres of preserved beauty.

When I arrive at the top, it's like stepping from Mitchell's time into the present. He would recognize most of the mountain, but not the summit. It features sidewalks and a viewing platform. Also, a parking lot: You can drive almost to the top.

A sign marks the highest point east of the Mississippi River — 6,684 feet. I stand next to that sign, on top of North Carolina, and I want to take it all in, just like Mitchell must have done more than 150 years ago. I want to see beauty, grandeur, and bigness in the distance. I see nothing but dense clouds above, in front of, below, and around me.

So much for the view.

I'm disappointed, but not really. I can look at pictures taken on clear days to see what I'm missing, but nothing can replicate what it's like to stand here. What's a mountain without clouds at the top?

I wanted to get to the top of Mount Mitchell to see, but I realize now that that leaves so much out. Climbing Mount Mitchell is a full-body experience: A pounding heart. Heaving lungs. Cool wind on my face. Adrenaline gives me a hiker's high equal to the altitude I've reached. As I walk from the sign to the viewing platform, no person from here to the Mississippi River stands closer to the sun than I do. I want to hang out at the top, bask in the moment. But I've learned from Mitchell: It's late, and I don't want to get caught up here in the dark.

But I've figured out what makes the top so special: Scaling Mount Mitchell makes me feel like part of the mountain. I climbed so close to the clouds that I felt like I stood among them. As I looked in awe at the opaque sky, I contributed to the silence. By reaching the summit, I became a very small part of some far-off person's vista, obscured though I might have been.

Elisha Mitchell is part of the mountain, too. He was buried here.

At the top. — *Matt Crossman*

MOUNT MITCHELL STATE PARK
2388 NC Highway 128, Burnsville, NC 28714
(828) 675-4611
ncparks.gov/mount-mitchell-state-park